The Best of
Wilfred Grenfell

Sir Wilfred Grenfell, 1865 - 1940

The *Best of*
Wilfred Grenfell

*Life and death stories from the skilled pen
of a legendary doctor of the North*

Edited by William Pope

NIMBUS CLASSICS

Nimbus Publishing Limited
3660 Strawberry Hill Street, Halifax, NS, B3K 5A9
(902) 455-4286 nimbus.ca

Printed and bound in Canada
NB0511

Library and Archives Canada Cataloguing in Publication

Grenfell, Wilfred Thomason, Sir, 1865-1940
The best of Wilfred Grenfell/selected and introduced
by William Pope.
First published: Hantsport, N.S. : Lancelot Press, 1990.
Includes bibliographical references.
ISBN 978-1-55109-581-3

1. Grenfell, Wilfred Thomason, Sir, 1865-1940. 2. Missionaries, Medical—Newfoundland and Labrador—Biography. 3. Labrador (N.L.)—Description and travel. 4. Labrador (N.L.)—Social life and customs. 5. Labrador (N.L.)—Biography. 6. Newfoundland and Labrador—Description and travel. 7. Newfoundland and Labrador —Social life and customs. 8. Newfoundland and Labrador—Biography. I. Pope, William, 1923- II. Title.
PS8513.R55A6 2006   610.69'5092   C2006-901996-7

Nimbus Publishing acknowledges the financial support for its publishing activities from the Government of Canada, the Canada Council for the Arts, and from the Province of Nova Scotia. We are pleased to work in partnership with the Province of Nova Scotia to develop and promote our creative industries for the benefit of all Nova Scotians.

CONTENTS

Introduction

"To believe is to do," Wilfred Grenfell said, and his 40 years as a medical missionary along the rugged Labrador coast amply illustrated his words. He was a prolific writer, fund raiser, and traveller, but it was his faith that empowered his life and gave it meaning; it enabled him to accomplish great tasks to the amazement of others and made him a legend even during his lifetime.

Sir Henry Richards, a close friend of Grenfell, tells of an occasion when they had gone out in a small sailing boat to visit some of the North Sea fishing vessels. A few miles off shore they encountered a terrific wind and huge waves. Richards became alarmed and suggested they turn back, but Grenfell replied: "What are you scared of? The Lord will look after us."

"He may look after you, Wilf," Richards cried out, "but how do you know he will look after me?"

Grenfell had a simple and uncomplicated faith — some called it naive — but this faith gave him a power and a boldness to innovate and to persevere. Funds had been found for a hospital ship, but a colleague did not think they should put the ship into operation until further money was found for its maintenance. This lack of funds never deterred Grenfell. He felt that if he was doing the Lord's work the required money would come. Others, even though they agreed there was urgent need for many of the projects Grenfell suggested, tried to restrain him. His Mission Board pleaded with him to have at least one half of the finances on hand before starting a new project. When Grenfell saw a need, however, he felt compelled to act. His faith never allowed doubt to enter his mind. Rather, it enabled him to concentrate on the issue at hand and to apply all his talents, his resourcefulness, medical skill, ability in dealing with people, and immense energy to a successful resolution of the problem.

Wilfred was born in 1865 in Parkgate, England, one of three sons. He grew up playing on the Sands of Dee. Nearby was the seaport of Chester, and at an early age he developed a love of the sea that remained with him throughout his life. Fishermen, to him, were heroes and ships that went out to sea were meeting with some grand challenge and adventure.

His father was a clergyman who for years was headmaster at the well regarded Mostyn House School for boys. When Wilfred was 18, his father left the school to accept a position as Chaplain at the London Hospital. A medical career appealed to Wilfred and he went with his parents to London and began his studies at the London Hospital Medical School. He did not distinguish himself there and, although a quick learner, he did not show the brilliance in scholarship of his father nor of his older brother Algernon. He seemed more interested in sports than studies and participated in boxing, cricket, football and rowing.

Brought up in a Christian home, he had compassion for the poor and sick but had no deep religious feelings until an event happened when he was 20 that was to change the direction of his life. Returning from a sick call one evening, he was attracted to a large tent where an evangelical meeting was being held. As he went in, he heard the words of a long, boring prayer, but suddenly another man, whom he later learned was Dwight L. Moody, jumped up, and said: "Let us sing a hymn while our brother finishes his prayer." In his message that night, Moody challenged his audience to follow Christ, to live as He would in their daily activities.

A dormant spiritual drive was aroused in Grenfell, and he immediately began to feel that his faith should be expressed in some tangible way. He talked to his mother, who was his lifelong confidant, about his experience, and she suggested he go to the Anglican vicar and offer his services. This pastor suggested he teach a Sunday School class. His pupils came from a rough district of the city, and Grenfell felt a boxing club would be more helpful to these boys than the traditional class teaching which was not going well. The vicar thought otherwise so Grenfell moved on. With others, he conducted street religious services and helped with a boys' club in which sport, including boxing, played a prominent role.

Dr. Frederick Treves, Surgeon at the London Hospital, called Grenfell an "indifferent" student and doctor. Nevertheless he saw a talent in the young man that he thought could be used constructively, and suggested he become a doctor with the National Mission to Deep Sea Fishermen.

Grenfell responded enthusiastically. He went to sea with the fishermen, moved among them as one of them, looked after their medical needs, and conducted devotional services. Before long this energetic doctor was made Superintendent of the North Sea Mission to Fishermen. Talkative, friendly, his mind filled with ideas, he attempted a number of schemes that would benefit the fishermen. He started a shore club at Gorleston where the men could relax, play games, and sing songs instead of associating with "loose" women and drinking too much alcohol which had been their custom.

News came to the Mission of the great need for medical services along the Labrador coast. The climate was harsh, the people poverty stricken, and living conditions had few refinements, but Grenfell eagerly volunteered for this work. His first contact with Labrador enchanted him. He marvelled at the beauty of sea and sky, of the bays and inlets, some fiord-like in appearance with rocky cliffs of great height rising almost perpendicular from the water. He urged the captain of his small ship to enter many of these waters but found him reluctant to do so because of the many shoals and unseen dangers in these unchartered seas. Grenfell promised himself that one day he would have his own boat and would visit these beautiful areas all along the coast.

Grenfell was no less impressed by the people of Labrador. They might be poor but they had a generous spirit. Grenfell would treat the sick in shack-like, isolated homes, and would be offered a cup of tea without milk or sugar because these commodities were lacking. Before leaving he would usually gather the family and any neighbors who might be nearby for a prayer and a Christian message. "I must tell the people why I have come," he would say to his medical associates, "so they too may know Christ in their daily lives." His sermons were made up of little stories taken from his own experiences along the coast that his hearers could identify with. To him religion was as natural as breathing, and he felt compelled to share the gospel of the Good News with others.

Always his beliefs must be expressed in good deeds, and his Christianity was ever seeking a practical expression. First came his medical work which saw four hospitals and eight nursing stations established as well as a hospital ship that journeyed along the coast. He founded a children's home, a sanatorium for tubercular patients, a farm, cooperative stores, and an active handicraft centre.

Fourteen years after his life had been changed by Dwight Moody's challenge to follow the Living Christ, Grenfell again met the evangelist in the United States. He told Moody how he had been influenced by his words that night in London. To Moody, as to Grenfell, faith was genuine only when it resulted in constructive action. A person's faith could be unerringly detected by examining his deeds. So Moody asked Grenfell: "What have you done since you heard me speak?" Grenfell described the service he was rendering to the people of Labrador. Moody was impressed by his faith and invited him to tell of his experiences at the evangelistic meetings he was then holding.

As Grenfell's work expanded in many directions, more funding was required, and he met this need by lecturing in the United States, England and Canada. Grenfell was not a great orator, but he chose dramatic material that he knew first-hand and he gave vivid descriptions of the impoverished lives of the people of Labrador. While his talks might ramble, sincerity shone through every word, and when he finished people gave him donations and some volunteered to go to Labrador to give him whatever service they could. Often committees were set up to attempt on-going assistance for the Grenfell work.

Grenfell always welcomed volunteer workers and valued their services. They might be trained or untrained people, but Grenfell felt every person should be given an opportunity to contribute to the work of the Mission.

Grenfell wrote hundreds of articles and authored thirty-three books, and one wonders where he found the time and energy to produce such a vast amount. In his writings, as in his lectures, he presented topics he knew intimately. He loved the majestic beauty of the isolated Labrador coast. To him it was an adventure to journey by dog team on a 20-mile trek to attend some patient. After medical attention had been given, and often after a prayer or a short service, he would sit down with the family for an hour or two to hear their stories. The material he gathered on these visits would later be used in his lectures and books, and for a man as loquacious as Grenfell it must have been a major achievement for him to sit back and patiently listen to their every day experiences. Still, Grenfell had a great affection for these people. He admired their generosity and courage and he saw adventure and drama in their daily battles to eke out a livelihood from the sea. Of his many books, *Adrift on an Ice Pan* has been his most popular and here, as in his other writings, he makes numerous spiritual observations while recounting a gripping story.

In *What Christ Means to Me*, Grenfell gave a more

complete account of his faith than in any of his other writings. He was 61 at the time and experiencing some heart trouble. Long periods spent in travel prevented him from consulting other books, but his mature spiritual reflections are presented in this short book with vigor and conviction. Grenfell never seemed to stop. His brain teemed with new ideas. He loved to be at the helm of his hospital ship responding to some urgent call. In his writings he enthusiastically told of the work he was doing with Christ in combatting great need. Less eagerly, but none the less faithfully, he travelled widely and raised vast sums of money through his lectures. Along the Labrador coast he was the beloved Doctor. Others might be as good or better medically than Grenfell, but no one else had his charismatic personality.

He had his eccentricities. As a young man crossing the ocean in a small ship, he was playing cricket on the deck and the last ball went overboard into the Atlantic. Immediately he requested that the Captain stop the boat so the ball could be retrieved. When the Captain refused, Grenfell jumped overboard. The Captain then had to turn his vessel around, and he saw the young doctor in the water with a big grin on his face and the ball in his hand. All his life Grenfell liked to take a morning dip in the sea even in ice-laden waters. Once when visiting a destitute family and learning the father had literally no clothes, he took off his own suit and gave it to the man and then proceeded to swim back to his hospital ship in his underwear. On his travels he was always inviting people to come to Labrador and help with the work. Sometimes these people would arrive when Grenfell was away and his associates would not know what to do with them.

No one could stay angry with Grenfell for long. His motives were good, his schemes, no matter how strange, were for the benefit of others, and he greeted people so warmly that little grievances were soon forgotten. He stimulated everyone around him. As the number of workers increased, from time to time personality problems arose but, when Grenfell came on the scene, his charm was irresistible and difficult situations were resolved harmoniously.

Grenfell was 43 years of age when he married. Returning from a lecture tour in England, he was sailing on the *Mauretania* to the United States where he was to receive an M.A. from Harvard and an LL.D. from Williams College. On board he met a beautiful girl and lost no time in proposing to her. She replied: "But you do not even know my name." He quickly responded: "That is not the issue. The only thing that interests me is what it is going to be."

However brief their courtship, the marriage was a great success. Wilfred adored his Anne, and she left the wealthy MacClanahan home in Chicago to share his adventurous life in Newfoundland and Labrador. While she did not fit in with the local people nearly so well as Grenfell, yet she was a strong personality, a good organizer, and she helped her husband in numerous ways. She was particularly adept in arranging his lecture tours, in introducing him to wealthy people, and in helping him to raise the ever-increasing funds that were needed to carry out the enlarging work.

Grenfell had a warm friendliness for the fisher folk, for his medical associates, and for other workers. He had the same ability to meet and make a favorable impression upon the rich and the famous, and he made friends with Teddy Roosevelt, Albert Schweitzer, Commander Robert E. Perry, Alexander Graham Bell, and Henry Ford. He came away from a visit with Andrew Carnegie with a gift of 3,000 books for his circulating library in Labrador.

A man as active as Grenfell in so many areas would inevitably run into opposition. The cooperative stores he started as an alternative to the wretched truck system that set the prices for fish and kept the fishermen perpetually in debt aroused the enmity of merchants. He waged a life-long battle against alcohol and was opposed by the liquor interests. He wanted non-denominational schools, and he ran into opposition from churches. Even the government of

Newfoundland criticized him bitterly for giving a too vivid picture in his lectures of destitute conditions in Labrador. When government leaders went to New England seeking investment funds for Newfoundland they were unsuccessful and blamed Grenfell for turning the investment community away with his tales of a bleak and impoverished people.

Wilfred Grenfell had his faults and his limitations, but these were overshadowed by his strengths, his faith, and his achievements. He inspired others with his own ideals. He recruited men and women of outstanding ability for positions of leadership in the Mission work, and such men as Drs. Little, Curtis, and Paton went on to make their own valuable contributions. He invited Jessie Luther to leave her work in Boston to teach handicrafts in St. Anthony, and the work she was encouraged to start has flourished to the present day.

Grenfell's herculean labors had an inevitable effect upon his health. He suffered a number of minor heart attacks, and his condition deteriorated to such an extent that by age sixty-nine he had to relinquish his active participation in the Labrador work. His devoted wife had a house built on Lake Champlain, Vermont, and in this quiet spot they spent their retirement years. Even then Grenfell travelled across the country to give lectures and Anne continued to raise money in various ways for the Grenfell Mission. In 1940, in the Vermont home, Grenfell died peacefully, his wife predeceasing him by two years. Their remains were both buried behind their old home in St. Anthony.

Grenfell tried to brighten the lives of isolated people. He not only provided medical services, but he did much to bring them into community living with more social relationships. Last summer I was privileged to visit his St. Anthony home and see something of his work that continues on beyond his own lifetime.

In his autobiography he states: "From my hill-top, I see more clearly that the value of a man's religion must be measured by what it has enabled him to do." His faith guided and empowered him in difficult areas of service. He felt God needed people to improve the world, to carry out His purposes, and it was his privilege and responsibility to respond whole-heartedly. To live as Christ would live was his ideal. This provided him with a life of deep joy and satisfaction, and he believed such a life would be continued, expanded and enriched as one left this earth for eternity.

In this volume an attempt has been made to present Grenfell through the vigor of his own words. His classic story, *Adrift on an Ice Pan*, is presented here in its entirety. He specifically wrote about his faith in *What Christ Means to Me*, and a lengthy extract is included. Several stories tell about conditions as he found them in Newfoundland and Labrador, and in his vivid accounts, such as, "That Christmas in Peace Haven," the struggle of the people to survive is heart-wrenching. A glimpse into his global travels is here recounted as is his marriage to Anne. Grenfell was a gifted writer, an excellent story-teller, and his writings still have the power to move and to inspire.

William Pope
President, Lancelot Press
October 18, 1990

Grenfell, travelling by kayak, passes an iceberg. "The boat, with such a force behind it of will power, would, I believe, have gone through anything."

1.
Adrift on an Ice Pan
Adrift on an Ice Pan, 1909

It was Easter Sunday at St. Anthony in the year 1908, but with us in northern Newfoundland still winter. Everything was covered with snow and ice. I was walking back after morning service, when a boy came running over from the hospital with the news that a large team of dogs had come from sixty miles to the southward, to get a doctor on a very urgent case. It was that of a young man on whom we had operated about a fortnight before for an acute bone disease in the thigh. The people had allowed the wound to close, the poisoned matter had accumulated, and we thought we should have to remove the leg. There was obviously, therefore, no time to be lost. So, having packed up the necessary instruments, dressings, and drugs, and having fitted out the dog-sleigh with my best dogs, I started at once, the messengers following me with their team.

My team was an especially good one. On many a long journey they had stood by me and pulled me out of difficulties by their sagacity and endurance. To a lover of his dogs, as every Christian man must be, each one had become almost as precious as a child to its mother. They were beautiful beasts: "Brin," the cleverest leader on the coast; "Doc," a large, gentle beast, the backbone of the team for power; "Spy," a wiry, powerful black and white dog; "Moody," a lop-eared black-

and-tan, in his third season, a plodder that never looked behind him; "Watch," the youngster of the team, long-legged and speedy, with great liquid eyes and a Gordon-setter coat; "Sue," a large, dark Eskimo, the image of a great black wolf, with her sharp-pointed and perpendicular ears, for she "harked back" to her wild ancestry; "Jerry," a large roan-colored slut, the quickest of all my dogs on her feet, and so affectionate that her overtures of joy had often sent me sprawling on my back; "Jack," a jet-black, gentle-natured dog, more like a retriever, that always ran next the sledge, and never looked back but everlastingly pulled straight ahead, running always with his nose to the ground.

It was late in April, when there is always the risk of getting wet through the ice, so that I was carefully prepared with spare outfit, which included a change of garments, snowshoes, rifle, compass, axe, and oilskin overclothes. The messengers were anxious that their team should travel back with mine, for they were slow at best and needed a lead. My dogs, however, being a powerful team, could not be held back, and though I managed to wait twice for their sleigh, I had reached a village about twenty miles on the journey before nightfall, and had fed the dogs, and was gathering a few people for prayers when they caught me up.

During the night the wind shifted to the northeast, which brought in fog and rain, softened the snow, and made travelling very bad, besides heaving a heavy sea into the bay. Our drive next morning would be somewhat over forty miles, the first ten miles on an arm of the sea, on salt-water ice.

In order not to be separated too long from my friends, I sent them ahead two hours before me, appointing a rendezvous in a log tilt that we have built in the woods as a halfway house. There is no one living on all that long coast-line, and to provide against accidents — which have happened more than once — we built this hut to keep dry clothing, food, and drugs in.

The first rain of the year was falling when I started, and I was obliged to keep on what we call the "ballicaters," or ice barricades, much farther up the bay than I had expected. The sea of the night before had smashed the ponderous covering of ice right to the landwash. There were great gaping chasms between the enormous blocks, which we call pans, and half a mile out it was all clear water.

An island three miles out had preserved a bridge of ice, however, and by crossing a few cracks I managed to reach it. From the island it was four miles across to a rocky promontory, — a course that would be several miles shorter than going round the shore. Here as far as the eye could reach the ice seemed good, though it was very rough. Obviously, it had been smashed up by the sea and then packed in again by the strong wind from the northeast, and I thought it had frozen together solid.

All went well till I was about a quarter of a mile from the landing-point. Then the wind suddenly fell, and I noticed that I was travelling over loose "sish," which was like porridge and probably many feet deep. By stabbing down, I could drive my whip handle through the thin coating of young ice that was floating on it. The sish ice consists of the tiny fragments where the large pans have been pounding together on the heavy sea, like the stones of Freya's grinding mill.

So quickly did the wind now come off shore, and so quickly did the packed "slob," relieved of the wind pressure, "run abroad," that already I could not see one pan larger than ten feet square; moreover, the ice was loosening so rapidly that I saw that retreat was absolutely impossible. Neither was there any way to get off the little pan I was surveying from.

There was not a moment to lose. I tore off my oilskins, threw myself on my hands and knees by the side of the komatik to give a larger base to hold, and shouted to my team to go ahead for the shore. Before we had gone twenty yards, the dogs got frightened, hesitated for a moment, and the komatik instantly sank into the slob. It was necessary then for the dogs to pull much harder, so that they now began to sink in also.

Earlier in the season the father of the very boy I was going to operate on had been drowned in this same way, his dogs tangling their traces around him in the slob. This flashed into my mind, and I managed to loosen my sheath-knife, scramble forward, find the traces in the water, and cut them, holding on to the leader's trace wound round my wrist.

Being in the water I could see no piece of ice that would bear anything up. But there was as it happened a piece of snow, frozen together like a large snowball, about twenty-five yards away, near where my leading dog, "Brin," was wallowing in the slob. Upon this he very shortly climbed, his long trace of ten fathoms almost reaching there before he went into the water.

This dog has weird black markings on his face, giving him the appearance of wearing a perpetual grin. After climbing out on the snow as if it were the most natural position in the world he deliberately shook the ice and water from his long coat, and then turned round to look for me. As he sat perched up there out of the water he seemed to be grinning with satisfaction. The other dogs were hopelessly bogged. Indeed, we were like flies in treacle.

Gradually, I hauled myself along that line that was still tied to my wrist, till without any warning the dog turned round and slipped out of his harness, and then once more turned his grinning face to where I was struggling.

It was impossible to make any progress through the sish ice by swimming, so I lay there and thought all would soon be over, only wondering if any one would ever know how it happened. There was no particular horror attached to it, and in fact I began to feel drowsy, as if I could easily go to sleep, when suddenly I saw the trace of another big dog that had himself gone through before he reached the pan, and though he was close to it was quite unable to force his way out. Along this I hauled myself, using him as a bow anchor, but much bothered by the other dogs as I passed them, one of which got on my shoulder, pushing me farther down into the ice. There was only a yard or so more when I had passed my living anchor, and soon I lay with my dogs around me on the little piece of slob ice. I had to help them on to it, working them through the lane that I had made.

The piece of ice we were on was so small it was obvious we must soon all be drowned, if we remained upon it as it drifted seaward into more open water. If we were to save our lives, no time was to be lost. When I stood up, I could see about twenty yards away a larger pan floating amidst the sish, like a great flat raft, and if we could get on to it we should postpone at least for a time the death that already seemed almost inevitable. It was impossible to reach it without a life line, as I had already learned to my cost, and the next problem was how to get one there. Marvellous to relate, when I had first fallen through, after I had cut the dogs adrift without any hope left of saving myself, I had not let my knife sink, but had fastened it by two half hitches to the back of one of the dogs. To my great joy there it was still, and shortly I was at work cutting all the sealskin traces still hanging from the dogs' harnesses, and splicing them together into one long line. These I divided and fastened to the backs of my two leaders, tying the near ends round my two wrists. I then pointed out to "Brin" the pan I wanted to reach and tried my best to make them go ahead, giving them the full length of my lines from two coils. My long sealskin moccasins, reaching to my thigh, were full of ice and water. These I took off and tied separately on the dogs' backs. My coat, hat, gloves, and overalls I had already lost. At first, nothing would induce the two dogs to move, and though I threw them off the pan two or three times, they struggled back upon it, which perhaps was only natural, because as soon as they fell through they could see nowhere else to make for. To me, however, this seemed to spell "the end." Fortunately, I had with me a small black spaniel, almost a featherweight, with large furry paws, called "Jack," who acts as my mascot and incidentally as my retriever. This at once flashed into my mind, and I felt I had still one more chance for life. So I spoke to him and showed him the direction, and then threw a piece of ice toward the desired goal. Without a moment's hesitation he

21

made a dash for it, and to my great joy got there safely, the tough scale of sea ice carrying his weight bravely. At once I shouted to him to "lie down," and this, too, he immediately did, looking like a little black fuzz ball on the white setting. My leaders could now see him seated there on the new piece of floe, and when once more I threw them off they understood what I wanted, and fought their way to where they saw the spaniel, carrying with them the line that gave me the one chance for my life. The other dogs followed them, and after painful struggling, all got out again except one. Taking all the run that I could get on my little pan, I made a dive, slithering with the impetus along the surface till once more I sank through. After a long fight, however, I was able to haul myself by the long traces on to this new pan, having taken care beforehand to tie the harnesses to which I was holding under the dogs' bellies, so that they could not slip them off. But alas! the pan I was now on was not large enough to bear us and was already beginning to sink, so this process had to be repeated immediately.

I now realized that, though we had been working toward the shore, we had been losing ground all the time, for the off-shore wind had already driven us a hundred yards farther out. But the widening gap kept full of the pounded ice, through which no man could possibly go.

I had decided I would rather stake my chances on a long swim even than perish by inches on the floe, as there was no likelihood whatever of being seen and rescued. But, keenly though I watched, not a streak even of clear water appeared, the interminable sish rising from below and filling every gap as it appeared. We were now resting on a piece of ice about ten by twelve feet, which, as I found when I came to examine it, was not ice at all, but simply snow-covered slob frozen into a mass, and I feared it would very soon break up in the general turmoil of the heavy sea, which was increasing as the ice drove off shore before the wind.

At first we drifted in the direction of a rocky point on which a heavy surf was breaking. Here I thought once again to swim ashore. But suddenly we struck a rock. A large piece broke off the already small pan, and what was left swung round in the backwash, and started right out to sea. There was nothing for it now but to hope for a rescue. Alas! there was little possibility of being seen. As I have already mentioned, no one lives around this big bay. My only hope was that the other komatik, knowing I was alone and had failed to keep my tryst, would perhaps come back to look for me. This, however, as it proved, they did not do.

The westerly wind was rising all the time, our coldest wind at this time of the year, coming as it does over the Gulf ice. It was tantalizing, as I stood with next to nothing on, the wind going through me and every stitch soaked in ice-water, to see my well-stocked komatik some fifty yards away. It was still above water, with food, hot tea in a thermos bottle, dry clothing, matches, wood, and everything on it for making a fire to attract attention.

It is easy to see a dark object on the ice in the daytime, for the gorgeous whiteness shows off the least thing. But the tops of bushes and large pieces of kelp have often deceived those looking out. Moreover, within our memory no man has been thus adrift on the bay ice. The chances were about one in a thousand that I should be seen at all, and if I were seen, I should probably be mistaken for some piece of refuse.

To keep from freezing, I cut off my long moccasins down to the feet, strung out some line, split the legs, and made a kind of jacket, which protected my back from the wind down as far as the waist. I have this jacket still, and my friends assure me it would make a good Sunday garment.

I had not drifted more than half a mile before I saw my poor komatik disappear through the ice, which was every minute loosening up into the small pans that it consisted of, and it seemed like a friend gone and one more tie with home and safety lost. To the northward, about a mile distant, lay the mainland along which I had passed so merrily in the morning, — only, it seemed, a few moments before.

By mid-day I had passed the island to which I had crossed on the ice bridge. I could see that the bridge was gone now. If I could reach the island I should only be marooned and destined to die of starvation. But there was little chance of that, for I was rapidly driving into the ever widening bay.

It was scarcely safe to move on my small ice raft, for fear of breaking it. Yet I saw I must have the skins of some of my dogs, — of which I had eight on the pan, — if I was to live the night out. There was now some three to five miles between me and the north side of the bay. There, immense pans of Arctic ice, surging to and fro on the heavy ground seas, were thundering into the cliffs like medieval battering-rams. It was evident that, even if seen, I could hope for no help from that quarter before night. No boat could live through the surf.

Unwinding the sealskin traces from my waist, round which I had wound them to keep the dogs from eating them, I made a slip-knot, passed it over the first dog's head, tied it round my foot close to his neck, threw him on his back, and stabbed him in the heart. Poor beast! I loved him like a friend, — a beautiful dog, — but we could not all hope to live. In fact, I had no hope any of us would, at that time, but it seemed better to die fighting.

In spite of my care the struggling dog bit me rather badly in the leg. I suppose my numb hands prevented my holding his throat as I could ordinarily do. Moreover, I must hold the knife in the wound to the end, as blood on the fur would freeze solid and make the skin useless. In this way I sacrificed two more large dogs, receiving only one more bite, though I fully expected that the pan I was on would break up in the struggle. The other dogs, who were licking their coats and trying to get dry, apparently took no notice of the fate of their comrades, — but I was very careful to prevent the dying dogs crying out, for the noise of fighting would probably have been followed by the rest attacking the down dog, and that was too close to me to be pleasant. A short shrift seemed to me better than a long one, and I envied the dead dogs whose troubles were over so quickly. Indeed, I came to balance in my mind whether, if once I passed into the open sea, it would not be better by far to use my faithful knife on myself than to die by inches. There seemed no hardship in the thought. I seemed fully to sympathize with the Japanese view of hara-kiri.

Working, however, saved me from philosophizing. By the time I had skinned these dogs, and with my knife and some of the harness had strung the skins together, I was ten miles on my way, and it was getting dark.

Away to the northward I could see a single light in the little village where I had slept the night before, where I had received the kindly hospitality of the simple fishermen in whose comfortable homes I have spent many a night. I could not help but think of them sitting down to tea, with no idea that there was any one watching them, for I had told them not to expect me back for three days.

Meanwhile I had frayed out a small piece of rope into oakum, and mixed it with fat from the intestines of my dogs. Alas, my match-box, which was always chained to me, had leaked, and my matches were in pulp. Had I been able to make a light, it would have looked so unearthly out there on the sea that I felt sure they would see me. But that chance was now cut off. However, I kept the matches, hoping that I might dry them if I lived through the night. While working at the dogs, about every five minutes I would stand up and wave my hands toward the land. I had no flag, and I could not spare my shirt, for, wet as it was, it was better than nothing in that freezing wind, and, anyhow, it was already nearly dark.

Unfortunately, the coves in among the cliffs are so placed that only for a very narrow space can the people in any house see the sea. Indeed, most of them cannot see it at all, so that I could not in the least expect any one to see me, even supposing it had been daylight.

Not daring to take any snow from the surface of my pan to break the wind with, I piled up the carcasses of my dogs. With my skin rug I could now sit down without getting soaked.

During these hours I had continually taken off all my clothes, wrung them out, swung them one by one in the wind, and put on first one and then the other inside, hoping that what heat there was in my body would thus serve to dry them. In this I had been fairly successful.

My feet gave me most trouble, for they immediately got wet again because my thin moccasins were easily soaked through on the snow. I suddenly thought of the way in which the Lapps who tend our reindeer manage for dry socks. They carry grass with them, which they ravel up and pad into their shoes. Into this they put their feet, and then pack the rest with more grass, tying up the top with a binder. The ropes of the harness for our dogs are carefully sewed all over with two layers of flannel in order to make them soft against the dogs' sides. So, as soon as I could sit down, I started with my trusty knife to rip up the flannel. Though my fingers were more or less frozen, I was able also to ravel out the rope, put it into my shoes, and use my wet socks inside my knicker-bockers, where, though damp, they served to break the wind. Then, tying the narrow strips of flannel together, I bound up the top of the moccasins, Lapp-fashion, and carried the bandage on up over my knee, making a ragged though most excellent puttee.

As to the garments I wore, I had opened recently a box of football clothes I had not seen for twenty years. I had found my old Oxford University football running shorts and a pair of Richmond Football Club red, yellow, and black stockings, exactly as I wore them twenty years ago. These with a flannel shirt and sweater vest were now all I had left. Coat, hat, gloves, oilskins, everything else, were gone, and I stood there in that odd costume, exactly as I stood twenty years ago on a football field, reminding me of the little girl of a friend, who, when told she was dying, asked to be dressed in her Sunday frock to go to heaven in. My costume, being very light, dried all the quicker, until afternoon. Then nothing would dry anymore, everything freezing stiff. It had been an ideal costume to struggle through the slob ice. I really believe the conventional garments missionaries are supposed to affect would have been fatal. My occupation till what seemed like midnight was unravelling rope, and with this I padded out my knickers inside, and my shirt as well, though it was a clumsy job, for I could not see what I was doing. Now, getting my largest dog, Doc, as big as a wolf and weighing ninety-two pounds, I made him lie down, so that I could cuddle round him. I then wrapped the three skins around me, arranging them so that I could lie on one edge, while the other came just over my shoulders and head.

My own breath collecting inside the newly flayed skin must have had a soporific effect, for I was soon fast asleep. One hand I had kept warm against the curled up dog, but the other, being gloveless, had frozen, and I suddenly awoke, shivering enough, I thought, to break my fragile pan. What I took at first to be the sun was just rising, but I soon found it was the moon, and then I knew it was about half-past twelve. The dog was having an excellent time. He hadn't been cuddled so warm all winter, and he resented my moving with low growls till he found it wasn't another dog.

The wind was steadily driving me now toward the open sea, and I could expect, short of a miracle, nothing but death out there. Somehow, one scarcely felt justified in praying for a miracle. But we have learned down here to pray for things we want, and, anyhow, just at that moment the miracle occurred. The wind fell off suddenly, and came with a light air from the southward, and then dropped stark calm. The ice was now "all abroad," which I was sorry for, for there was a big safe pan not twenty yards away from me. If I could have got on that, I might have killed my other dogs when the time came, and with their coats I could hope to hold out for two or three days more, and with the food and drink their bodies would offer me need not at least die of hunger or thirst. To tell the truth, they were so big and strong I was half afraid to tackle them with only a sheath-knife on my small and unstable raft.

But it was now freezing hard. I knew the calm water

between us would form into cakes, and I had to recognize that the chance of getting near enough to escape on to it was gone. If, on the other hand, the whole bay froze solid again I had yet another possible chance. For my pan would hold together longer and I should be opposite another village, called Goose Cove, at daylight, and might possibly be seen from there. I knew that the komatiks there would be starting at daybreak over the hills for a parade of Orangemen about twenty miles away. Possibly, therefore, I might be seen as they climbed the hills. So I lay down, and went to sleep again.

It seems impossible to say how long one sleeps, but I woke with a sudden thought in my mind that I must have a flag; but again I had no pole and no flag. However, I set to work in the dark to disarticulate the legs of my dead dogs, which were now frozen stiff, and which were all that offered a chance of carrying anything like a distress signal. Cold as it was, I determined to sacrifice my shirt for that purpose with the first streak of daylight.

It took a long time in the dark to get the legs off, and when I had patiently marled them together with old harness rope and the remains of the skin traces, it was the heaviest and crookedest flag-pole it has ever been my lot to see. I had had no food from six o'clock the morning before, when I had eaten porridge and bread and butter. I had, however, a rubber band which I had been wearing instead of one of my garters, and I chewed that for twenty-four hours. It saved me from thirst and hunger, oddly enough. It was not possible to get a drink from my pan, for it was far too salty. But anyhow that thought did not distress me much, for as from time to time I heard the cracking and grinding of the newly formed slob, it seemed that my devoted boat must inevitably soon go to pieces.

At last the sun rose, and the time came for the sacrifice of my shirt. So I stripped, and, much to my surprise, found it not half so cold as I had anticipated. I now re-formed my dog-skins with the raw side out, so that they made a kind of coat quite rivalling Joseph's. But, with the rising of the sun, the frost came out of the joints of my dogs' legs, and the friction caused by waving it made my flag-pole almost tie itself in knots. Still, I could raise it three or four feet above my head, which was very important.

Now, however, I found that instead of being as far out at sea as I had reckoned, I had drifted back in a northwesterly direction, and was off some cliffs known as Ireland Head. Near these there was a little village looking seaward, whence I should certainly have been seen. But, as I had myself, earlier in the winter, been night-bound at this place, I had learnt there was not a single soul living there at all this winter. The people had all, as usual, migrated to the winter houses up the bay, where they get together for schooling and social purposes.

I soon found it was impossible to keep waving so heavy a flag all the time, and yet I dared not sit down, for that might be the exact moment some one would be in a position to see me from the hills. The only thing in my mind was how long I could stand up and how long go on waving that pole at the cliffs. Once or twice I thought I saw men against their snowy faces, which, I judged, were about five and a half miles from me, but they were only trees. Once, also, I thought I saw a boat approaching. A glittering object kept appearing and disappearing on the water, but it was only a small piece of ice sparkling in the sun as it rose on the surface. I think that the rocking of my cradle up and down on the waves had helped me to sleep, for I felt as well as ever I did in my life; and with the hope of a long sunny day, I felt sure I was good to last another twenty-four hours, — if my boat would hold out and not rot under the sun's rays.

Each time I sat down to rest, my big dog "Doc" came and kissed my face and then walked to the edge of the ice-pan, returning again to where I was huddled up, as if to say, "Why don't you come along? Surely it is time to start." The other dogs also were now moving about very restlessly, occasionally trying to satisfy their hunger by gnawing at the dead bodies of their brothers.

I determined, at mid-day, to kill a big Eskimo dog and drink his blood, as I had read only a few days before in *Farthest North* of Dr. Nansen's doing, — that is, if I survived the battle with him. I could not help feeling, even then, my ludicrous position, and I thought, if ever I got ashore again, I should have to laugh at myself standing hour after hour waving my shirt at those lofty cliffs, which seemed to assume a kind of sardonic grin, so that I could almost imagine they were laughing at me. At times I could not help thinking of the good breakfast that my colleagues were enjoying at the back of these same cliffs, and of the snug fire and the comfortable room which we call our study.

I can honestly say that from first to last not a single sensation of fear entered my mind, even when I was struggling in the slob ice. Somehow it did not seem unnatural; I had been through the ice half a dozen times before. For the most part I felt very sleepy, and the idea was then very strong in my mind that I should soon reach the solution of the mysteries that I had been preaching about for so many years.

Only the previous night (Easter Sunday) at prayers in the cottage, we had been discussing the fact that the soul was entirely separate from the body, that Christ's idea of the body as the temple in which the soul dwells is so amply borne out by modern science. We had talked of thoughts from that admirable book *Brain and Personality*, by Dr. Thompson of New York, and also of the same subject in the light of a recent operation performed at the Johns Hopkins Hospital by Dr. Harvey Cushing. The doctor had removed from a man's brain two large cystic tumors without giving the man an anaesthetic, and the patient had kept up a running conversation with him all the while the doctor's fingers were working in his brain. It had seemed such a striking proof that ourselves and our bodies are two absolutely different things.

Our eternal life has always been with me a matter of faith. It seems to me one of those problems that must always be a mystery to knowledge. But my own faith in this matter had been so untroubled that it seemed now almost natural to be leaving through this portal of death from an ice-pan. In many ways, also, I could see how a death of this kind might be of value to the particular work that I am engaged in. Except for my friends, I had nothing I could think of to regret whatever. Certainly, I should like to have told them the story. But then one does not carry folios of paper in running shorts which have no pockets, and all my writing gear had gone by the board with the komatik.

I could still see a testimonial to myself some distance away in my khaki overalls, which I had left on another pan in the struggle of the night before. They seemed a kind of company, and would possibly be picked up and suggest the true story. Running through my head all the time, quite unbidden, were the words of the old hymn:

"My God, my Father, while I stray
Far from my home on life's dark way,
Oh, teach me from my heart to say,
    Thy will be done!"

It is a hymn we hardly ever sing out here, and it was an unconscious memory of my boyhood days.

It was a perfect morning, — a cobalt sky, an ultramarine sea, a golden sun, an almost wasteful extravagance of crimson over hills of purest snow, which caught a reflected glow from rock and crag. Between me and the hills lay miles of rough ice and long veins of thin black slob that had formed during the night. For the foreground there was my poor, gruesome pan, bobbing up and down on the edge of the open sea, stained with blood, and littered with carcasses and debris. It was smaller than last night, and I noticed also that the new ice from the water melted under the dogs' bodies had been formed at the expense of its thickness. Five dogs, myself in colored football costume, and a bloody dogskin cloak, with a gay flannel shirt on a pole of frozen dogs' legs, completed the picture. The sun was almost hot by now, and I was conscious of a surplus of heat in my skin coat. I began to look longingly at one of my remaining dogs, for an appetite will rise even on an ice-pan, and that made me think of fire. So once again I inspected my matches. Alas! the heads were in paste, all but three or four blue-top wax ones.

These I now laid out to dry, while I searched about on my snow-pan to see if I could get a piece of transparent ice to make a burning-glass. For I was pretty sure that with all the unravelled tow I had stuffed into my leggings, and with the fat of my dogs, I could make smoke enough to be seen if only I could get a light. I had found a piece which I thought would do, and had gone back to wave my flag, which I did every two minutes, when I suddenly thought I saw again the glitter of an oar. It did not seem possible, however, for it must be remembered it was not water which lay between me and the land, but slob ice, which a mile or two inside me was very heavy. Even if people had seen me, I did not think they could get through, though I knew that the whole shore would then be trying. Moreover, there was no smoke rising on the land to give me hope that I had been seen. There had been no gun-flashes in the night, and I felt sure that, had any one seen me, there would have been a bonfire on every hill to encourage me to keep going.

So I gave it up, and went on with my work. But the next time I went back to my flag, the glitter seemed very distinct, and though it kept disappearing as it rose and fell on the surface, I kept my eyes strained upon it, for my dark spectacles had been lost, and I was partly snowblind.

I waved my flag as high as I could raise it, broadside on. At last, beside the glint of the white oar, I made out the black streak of the hull. I knew that, if the pan held on for another hour, I should be all right.

With that strange perversity of the human intellect, the first thing I thought of was what trophies I could carry with my luggage from the pan, and I pictured the dog-bone flagstaff adorning my study. (The dogs actually ate it afterwards.) I thought of preserving my ragged puttees with our collection of curiosities. I lost no time now at the burning-glass. My whole mind was devoted to making sure I should be seen, and I moved about as much as I dared on the raft, waving my sorry token aloft.

At last there could be no doubt about it: the boat was getting nearer and nearer. I could see that my rescuers were frantically waving, and, when they came within shouting distance, I heard some one cry out, "Don't get excited. Keep on the pan where you are." They were infinitely more excited than I. Already to me it seemed just as natural now to be saved as, half an hour before, it had seemed inevitable I should be lost, and had my rescuers only known, as I did, the sensation of a bath in that ice when you could not dry yourself afterwards, they need not have expected me to follow the example of the apostle Peter and throw myself into the water.

As the man in the bow leaped from the boat on to my ice raft and grasped both my hands in his, not a word was uttered. I could see in his face the strong emotions he was trying hard to force back, though in spite of himself tears trickled down his cheeks. It was the same with each of the others of my rescuers, nor was there any reason to be ashamed of them. These were not the emblems of weak sentimentality, but the evidences of the realization of the deepest and noblest emotion of which the human heart is capable, the vision that God has use for us his creatures, the sense of that supreme joy of the Christ, — the joy of unselfish service. After the hand shake and swallowing a cup of warm tea that had been thoughtfully packed in a bottle, we hoisted in my remaining dogs and started for home. To drive the boat home there were not only five Newfoundland fishermen at the oars, but five men with Newfoundland muscles in their backs, and five as brave hearts as ever beat in the bodies of human beings.

So, slowly but steadily, we forged through to the shore, now jumping out on to larger pans and forcing them apart with the oars, now hauling the boat out and dragging her over, when the jam of ice packed tightly in by the rising wind was impossible to get through otherwise.

My first question, when at last we found our tongues, was, "How ever did you happen to be out in the boat in this ice?" To my astonishment they told me that the previous night four men had been away on a long headland cutting out some dead harp seals that they had killed in the fall and left to freeze up in a rough wooden store they had built there, and that as they were leaving for home, my pan of ice had drifted out clear of Hare Island, and one of them, with his keen fisherman's eyes, had seen something unusual. They at once returned to their village, saying there was something alive drifting out to sea on the floe ice. But their report had been discredited, for the people thought that it could be only the top of some tree.

All the time I had been driving along I knew that there was one man on that coast who had a good spyglass. He tells me he instantly got up in the midst of his supper, on hearing the news, and hurried over the cliffs to the lookout, carrying his trusty spy-glass with him. Immediately, dark as it was, he saw that without any doubt there was a man out on the ice. Indeed, he saw me wave my hands every now and again towards the shore. By a very easy process of reasoning on so uninhabited a shore, he at once knew who it was, though some of the men argued that it must be someone else. Little had I thought, as night was closing in, that away on that snowy hilltop lay a man with a telescope patiently searching those miles of ice for *me*. Hastily they rushed back to the village and at once went down to try to launch a boat, but that proved to be impossible. Miles of ice lay between them and me, the heavy sea was hurling great blocks on the landwash, and night was already falling, the wind blowing hard on shore.

The whole village was aroused, and messengers were despatched at once along the coast, and lookouts told off to all the favorable points, so that while I considered myself a laughing-stock, bowing with my flag to those unresponsive cliffs, there were really many eyes watching me. One man told me that with his glass he distinctly saw me waving the shirt flag. There was little slumber that night in the villages, and even the men told me there were few dry eyes, as they thought of the impossibility of saving me from perishing. We are not given to weeping over much on this shore, but there are tears that do a man honor.

Before daybreak this fine volunteer crew had been gotten together. The boat, with such a force behind it of will power, would, I believe, have gone through anything. And, after seeing the heavy breakers through which we were guided, loaded with their heavy ice battering rams, when at last we ran through the harbor-mouth with the boat on our return, I knew well what wives and children had been thinking of when they saw their loved ones put out. Only two years ago I remember a fisherman's wife watching her husband and three sons take out a boat to bring in a stranger that was showing flags for a pilot. But the boat and its occupants have not yet come back.

Every soul in the village was on the beach as we neared the shore. Every soul was waiting to shake hands when I landed. Even with the grip that one after another gave me, some no longer trying to keep back the tears, I did not find out my hands were frost-burnt, — a fact I have not been slow to appreciate since, however. I must have been a weird sight as I stepped ashore, tied up in rags, stuffed out with oakum, wrapped in the bloody skins of dogs, with no hat, coat, or gloves besides, and only a pair of short knickers. It must have seemed to some as if it were the old man of the sea coming ashore.

But no time was wasted before a pot of tea was exactly where I wanted it to be, and some hot stew was locating itself where I had intended an hour before the blood of one of my remaining dogs should have gone.

Rigged out in the warm garments that fishermen wear, I started with a large team as hard as I could race for the hospital, for I had learnt that the news had gone over that I was lost. It was soon painfully impressed upon me that I could not much enjoy the ride, for I had to be hauled like a log up the hills, my feet being frost-burnt so that I could not walk. Had I guessed this before going into the house, I might have avoided much trouble.

It is time to bring this egotistic narrative to an end. "Jack" lies curled up by my feet while I write this short account. "Brin" is once again leading and lording it over his fellows. "Doc" and the other survivors are not forgotten, now that we have again returned to the less romantic episodes of a mission hospital life. There stands in our hallway a bronze tablet to the memory of three noble dogs, Moody, Watch, and Spy, whose lives were given for mine on the ice. In my home in England my brother has placed a duplicate tablet, and has added these words, "Not one of them is forgotten before your Father which is in heaven." And this I most fully believe to be true. The boy whose life I was intent on saving was brought to the hospital a day or two later in a boat, the ice having cleared off the coast not to return for that season. He was operated on successfully, and is even now on the high road to recovery. We all love life. I was glad to be back once more with possibly a new lease of it before me. I had learned on the pan many things, but chiefly that the one cause for regret, when we look back on a life which we think is closed forever, will be the fact that we have wasted its opportunities. As I went to sleep that first night there still rang in my ears the same verse of the old hymn which had been my companion on the ice, "Thy will, not mine, O Lord."

"A sudden clear glimpse of the fox betrayed the dark, glossy coat of that doyen of our northern furs, a black silver."

2.
That Christmas in Peace Haven

That Christmas in Peace Haven, 1923

The trouble with this particular Christmas was that it came after such a "total blank" in our fisheries that, far from expecting Santa Claus, it was absolutely certain that some of our folk would be looking for "a bit o' loaf."

The salmon-fishermen in the bay had not more than a hundred tierce between them, and British Columbian salmon had cut the price as well. Our beautiful trout was temporarily a drug in the market, and had hardly paid the cost of salt and cooperage. Not a deer had come to the landwash to help the larder, and, owing to the necessity of devoting every moment to the fishery, the usual time for an early fall hunt had been allowed to slip by. The only plentiful creatures in the country seemed to be the mice and the lemmings. But that fact augured ill for our last resource, the fur-trapping, for foxes won't come out to the landwash if they can get food in the country, and marten and mink won't take bait when there is no need for them to run risks.

Yet when I ran into Peace Haven in the late fall to leave a box of supplies for the doctor on his winter journeys, you would never have thought there was anything but the jolliest of Christmases ahead for the good people round the little harbor.

The patriarch of the place, Uncle Joe, expressed the general good sense by saying, "Well, youse see, Doctor, troubles hurts just that much less if you don't go to meet them till they comes after you."

It so happened that Jake Kelsom's little boy was sick and that had stirred Jake's mind, because it was acutely visible. He had come some two miles across the hills from a neighboring harbor for help. "I see'd t' smoke, Doctor, as you rounded Fishing Point Head," he said, "and t' ole missis thought maybe you'd come over and see our Jakie."

It was late before we reached his house, and only just not too late for Jakie.

"It will mean staying here for the night, and perhaps taking Jakie with us to-morrow," I said to the anxious man. "Can you give me a shake-down for the night?"

" 'Deed us can, Doctor. T' ole missis'll fix up t' room for you."

There was only dry bread for supper, and tea with a drop of molasses, and I had omitted to put anything but medical supplies into my "nonny bag."

"It's only poor fare us can offer you," Jake apologized. "But it's hard times t' year."

"As long as you have enough flour not to starve, and can get some fat, you'll be all right, Jake, till the ducks come south. Perhaps you can kill a deer, too."

"That's just the trouble," replied my host. "We're on our last barrel now, and God knows where the next is to come from. Mr. Roper have shut up t' store at Brandy Harbor for t' winter. He says he can't afford to give credit, and he 'lows us won't be getting anything to buy un with."

Noticing just then that his mouthpiece was an empty pipe, I handed him my tobacco-pouch. The smile which spread over his face repaid me for the fill, and for the half-pound more which I later sent over from the ship's stock. A couple of curly-headed youngsters of four and five were on the floor playing with two old cotton spools in absolute contentment. The shortage of soap even had not in the least affected their equanimity, much less the eccentricity of their garments.

As we sat in silence, puffing at our pipes, my thoughts went awing, and from the heights I seemed to get a view of all men as children, forgetting the higher joys of manhood in playing with toys, and it made me want to help my fellow in distress.

I was suddenly brought back from the clouds by a knock at the door. On opening it, there stood a man with a large tin baking-pan in his hand. He seemed somewhat confused at seeing a stranger in the house, and after toying with the pan for a minute was evidently about to beat a retreat.

"Come in, Tom," sang out my host. " 'Tis is only t' doctor, Come right in."

Tom closed the door and came forward somewhat sheepishly to shake hands. Meanwhile, without a word's having passed between them, Jake rose and, seizing the baking-pan, removed it to the proximity of his last barrel of flour, from which he promptly proceeded to fill it "chockablock." As he returned and gave it to its owner, I noticed the same kind of look light up Tom's face as I had previously seen on my host's.

As soon as he had gone, Jake tried to excuse his soft-heartedness by saying first that it was only a loan. But he spoiled that statement by adding, "One baking more or less won't make much difference, will it?"

"Perhaps it will make more than you think," I replied; " 'there is that which withholdeth and yet maketh poor.' "

We turned in soon after, and I found no difficulty in diagnosing that my needy friend slept far more soundly than I.

A heavy nor'easter with fog outside kept us in Peace Haven another day. I was soon satisfied that, however good my intention, it was far beyond my capacity adequately to relieve the situation. What we could do was cheerfully done, but when we came to get up our anchor for sailing, I felt badly over even the few guns the good-hearted folk fired to give us a

41

"send-off," for I knew how scarce a load of powder was, and that each discharge might mean a duck less for the cooking-pot.

There have been similar cases in my experience when somehow the windows of heaven seemed to open to supply the people's needs. But this was not one of those occasions. On the contrary, all the friends alike, including even Uncle Joe, only just "scrabbled along." By the first of December, the little community was almost at its wit's end to know what to do for food. They had all moved up the bay now to their winter cottages to get the protection of the trees from the winds which make life on the islands and even on the outer land almost unbearable. Some of the families had been lucky enough to strike a head of caribou and had secured a supply of venison. But among these fortunate ones were neither of my straitened friends. These two men were furring together — that is, they shared the same fur path and halved all they caught, an arrangement due to the small number of traps either of them could afford to purchase.

It had come Tom Marvin's turn to visit the "path." The snow was now lying deep on the ground, and the nose and ears of even a well-fed man needed careful tending in that atmosphere. Tom was on half rations, and "dry flour ain't much to start a day's work on." But, clad in the best he could find to keep out the weather, he started on his long tramp. Mile after mile went by; trap after trap was examined. But always the same tale repeated itself. The trap was frozen over, or drifted over, but never a sign of a living animal nigh any of them. On and on he plodded till he had reached the very farthest trap tailed. Lo and behold, it was gone, and not a sign to be seen of it. There was a layer of young snow on the ground hiding even the most recent tracks, and the light wind that was blowing had drifted them all over. Poor Tom was weak from want of good food and worn out from the journey as well. This last disappointment seemed to take the last bit of grit out of him. This particular trap had been tailed, as he knew, on the top of an old stump which they had fixed in a very narrow part of the pathway. The stump had been selected to prevent the trap from being snowed deep under. If only he could find that stump, he might be able to get some clue as to the whereabouts of his trap. Pulling himself together, he staggered on in search of it. "You see, Doctor," he said afterwards, "I wa'n't quite myself, perhaps, just then, or I wouldn't have missed the spot."

As it was, he came back twice on his tracks before, just under the surface of the snow, his foot struck the stump. Lying down and blowing away the dry, powdery snow, he was able to make out three things: first, the trap had gone, chain and all, the staple having been drawn out of the old stump; secondly, it was a fox that had taken it away; and thirdly, it had gone within the last twenty-four hours. But where had it gone, and could he find it? On every side could be seen snow, snow, nothing but snow, — except that here and there a few green tops of some scant spruce trees which we call "tuckamore" peeped out. The excitement of the hope bred of the knowledge of his find had almost made a new man of him. He tried every art he knew to guide him as to the way to go. But after starting in all four directions and circling round and round with the post as a center, weary and disheartened, he felt he must give it up.

Already night was coming on. What would be the use of even a silver to him if he perished in getting it. He was cold and he was hungry. He had already drawn heavily on his reserve of strength.

Yes, he would give it up. Just as well to die one way as another. What was the use of struggling against such odds any longer? He had almost turned to strike out for home, when the vision of his two curly-headed lads crying with hunger that he was powerless to appease, and the sad face of his young wife rose so vividly before him that he turned once again. "God help me! it's better to perish alone than to see 'em suffer." And once again he set out blindly on the quest.

Heading for the nearest clumps of tuckamore, he carefully

examined the ground all about, but found no signs. He set off once more, closely scrutinizing drogue after drogue, as we call these small clumps of trees. On and on he wandered till suddenly a white mark like a fresh trail-blaze, low down on a young fir, caught his watchful eye. A closer examination showed that the bark had been notched by some sharp instrument — and in a moment more he was certain that some animal carrying a trap had been seeking shelter in the thicket. But there was none there now, and which way was he to go? What was he to do next? The land to the north of him was steep, rising eventually at the top to a jagged wilderness of high pinnacled rocks. To the southward it fell away in a long even slope to a large lake. The chances were all in favor of the fox having sought the shelter of the rocks. But there was no visible track. It might be exactly the wrong direction. The torturing dilemma nearly drove him crazy. Wouldn't it be as well to take the easier path? But he decided to play the game to the finish. Without exactly knowing why, or even how he got along, he began to climb the shoulder of the hill. He had not gone more than half a mile, when, as he topped the level of a low ridge, he thought he saw, away above him on the snow, a tiny black speck moving. A second more and he was sure of it.

Now began a race for life. His will was working at its best. He was really crazy now, but it was with tumultuous hope and maddening excitement. The memory of fatigue, the fear of perishing alone, everything in heaven and earth had vanished from his consciousness. There on the hill above him and almost within his very grasp was the price of food for his loved ones. But with every second the gap was widening. Once the fox should gain the craggy summit there would be no hope of getting him. Tom was a great runner, and at any other time the issue would not have been in doubt for five minutes. But his will had flogged the willing muscles into action to the very limit of their power; their reserve was exhausted. Even as he started on the chase, his snowshoe caught in an unnoticed snag and he stumbled and fell. When he rose there was a dizziness in his head which prevented his seeing the speck. However, an agony of fear like the prick of a big spur sent him stumbling along again. Another minute, and he sighted the speck moving away far above him on the hillside.

Fortunately for Tom, it was a handicap race all round. The wretched fox, flying for his life, had to drag the heavy trap on his leg. He was stumbling and falling scarcely less frequently than his competitor in the race. Already the goal was in view and it seemed as though the fox, as well as the man, recognized the winning-post, and each was straining every nerve to get an advantage. Now the man would gain, till a slip of his snowshoe in the rapidly increasing incline, or a further stumble from carelessness and exhaustion, again made him lose ground. Now the trailing trap, catching in a snag, would trip up the fox for a second with a round turn, and he would lose time snarling and biting at it. A couple of hundred yards ahead loomed the tangled labyrinth of huge rocks, torn by the iron foot of our winters from the massive peak that formed the summit of the hill above, — a huge moraine with endless rocky fortresses, a very plethora of cities of refuge, from any one of which the fugitive was well aware he could bark defiance at his enemy. On the whole, the man was gaining, but not fast enough to give him the victory, and without his realizing it, the fact was telling against him. At this moment a new element entered the arena. A sudden clear glimpse of the fox betrayed the dark, glossy coat of that *doyen* of our northern furs, a black silver. This is the prize of the North. With its capture the trapper not only wins his knightly spurs, but also money enough to keep him without fear of want for many a day to come.

Here was a man, himself half-fed and half-clad, his loved ones perishing by inches for the want of mere necessities at home, his future so black that he greatly preferred death to facing it, and here, almost in his hands, but yet slipping from his grasp, was food, clothing, rest from anxiety, and all he needed to make life contented.

A madman is said to be capable of sudden superhuman

45

feats of strength, the ill control of his nerve impulses making it possible for him to let every reserve go at the same moment. As Tom told me the story afterward, there was only one explanation of what happened. He must have gone stark mad. All he remembers was that something, he doesn't know what, shot him forward up that last incline like an arrow from a bow. He recalls that somehow his snowshoes did not hold as the angle of the hill became too steep. But in spite of that on and on he went. He remembers the fox as it got into the mouth of a great cleft, turning and yelping at him, and that with one big jump he flung himself bodily upon it. And then oblivion.

When he came to himself it was dark. At first he forgot where he was. He was miserably cold, his head was dizzy and aching, he was in the open, lying on the snow. Surely he had gone to sleep by mistake. There was something wet on his head. He put his hand to it, and examined it by the reflection of the moonlight — blood. Something must have hit him. Probably a rock had rolled down on him. Then suddenly his hand touched something cold which stuck fast to his wet finger, burning it like a red-hot iron. He tore it off and with it a piece of skin from his hand. But he felt no pain. A chain! What could a chain be doing there? A chain! Then suddenly it all flashed back into his mind: the misery at home, the tramp, the lost trap, the struggle. But the fox — where was the fox? He tried to rise, but could not. So he crawled up on his feet against the face of the big rock, and stood for a moment swaying in the moonlight. Then, dropping on his knees in the snow, in an agony of unspoken supplication, he groped in under the rock to find if possibly the fox might still be there. Nothing but snow and rock met his touch. He listened, but no sound could be heard. It must have slipped the trap while he was unconscious, or perhaps gnawed itself free. Dizziness was overcoming Tom and the night was getting darker.

He was too weak to hope to get home, and the savage comfort came to his mind, "Well, it won't make any difference to me that I lost him"; and once more he sank down into his old place on the snow. Ugh! What was that? The chain again. He tore at it in mad anger to try and hurl it from him. But no, it would not move. He grabbed it in both hands and in senseless rage flung his weight into the strain. It gave slowly. It was fast to something: the trap, of course. Why hadn't he thought of that? At least, it should deceive no one else. He would hurl it into this rocky fastness where no one could ever find it — to lure another man to his undoing. But even as it came, a great heap of snow came with it, and, flinging his arms around it, Tom once more rose from his knees as he prepared to hurl it from him. But what was that? Surely God Almighty wouldn't mock him now. The snow was soft in his arms, yet it certainly was hard in lumps. Something was projecting: a frozen stick. No, it wasn't that; it was hairy. Once more he reeled and fell on the snow, as he realized that he held in his arms the dead body of the black fox.

Exactly what followed is very hazy in his memory. Something had made him stronger. He supposes it was the unconquerable determination to tell the good news. At first he pictured himself going straight home, and opening the door, with the fox in his arms. His strength seemed like that of ten as he thought of the look on his wife's face, and of the children when they found what it meant to them. No more hunger, no more of the awful anxiety which was worse than hunger. He thought of Jake's joy and what he would say first. It was Jake who had fed him when he was hungry. He loved Jake with a man's whole love. Oh! he could get back all right. He must get back if he fell dead at his own door.

Cuddling the fox like a baby, he was able to get on his feet and start down the hill. The next thing he remembers was picking himself up out of some tuckamores into which he had wandered. That reminded him. The tilt, the mailman's tilt in the green rudge could be only a short distance away. Of course he couldn't get back as he was. He must get shelter till morning. It was trees he needed; trees to shelter him. The tilt! Why hadn't he thought of it! And, once more climbing to his feet, he stumbled on into the night, clinging to his precious burden like a drowning man.

Elsie, his wife, had been anxious when he set out. She knew he wasn't his real self. Only because it was as bad to stay as to go had she consented. She had persuaded him not to carry his gun. It was too heavy for him on such a long round. She needed it to fire for him if he was late. They all said there was no use in it, as there wasn't a rabbit around, and besides it might frighten away foxes from the path. All the coast knew that Mark Gulliver had shot himself a year or two before, when his family were starving. Now she was glad she had kept it. She'd go over and see Jake. Jake would certainly know where to look for him even if night had overtaken him. And Jake — why, he'd go anywhere at any time for anybody, much more for Tom.

Bertie and Johnnie were given a rather larger piece of bread — the merest smear of molasses disguised it. There had been no kerosene for a light for weeks, and sleep kept them from thinking of hunger. Only half-satisfied, the children had cried themselves to sleep in their deep wooden bunks, before she locked their door and slipped over to Jake's house.

"Said he'd be back early, did he?" said Jake in his kindly way as poor Elsie explained her fears to him. "Well, sure it's early yet if it is a bit dark. But I 'lows he's changed his mind and is going to sleep in a tilt to-night."

"But he promised he wouldn't," urged the woman. "He promised, hit or miss, he wouldn't leave me alone to-night. I can't bear it, Jake. I tell you I can't bear it. If he doesn't get back by ten o'clock, I'm going to ask Jessie to let me bring the boys over. I must go after him. I can't stay here, and he perishing."

"He won't perish, lass," Jake answered; "there's a thousand things as 'ud make him stay on the path."

"I tell you, Jake, he's in trouble. I know it as sure as I'm standing here. If he isn't back by ten, may I bring Bertie and Johnnie over?"

"Yes, and welcome," he answered. "But if it comes to going, why, you'd better let me go."

"No, no," she replied. "I know the way the path runs, and if any one can find him, why, I can, if so be he's lost."

The cheap wooden clock still pointed far from ten when once more Elsie trudged over to Jake's with her bundle, one lad trotting beside her. Though Jake was himself all ready, there was no dissuading Elsie from going also.

"Jake," she said, "since I left you, I'm sure something's wrong with Tom. I didn't see him, but I heard him. He's out on the snow, and he wants me. I've got some bread here and a little bit of raw tea. There's nothing else in the house now." And unbidden tears welled in her eyes as she thought of the little she could give the husband of her love if she did find him.

"Don't fret, lass," said Jake. "I've put in a small bottle of molasses. 'T is a pity there be no fat. But it's no good crying over it." And, seeing she was determined to go, he said no more, but started out with her.

It was getting light before they had visited their own ten-mile tilt, only to find it empty. Fortunately there was no wind, so that when this strange couple reached the spot where the last trap had been tailed, they had a complete riddle written in the snow to solve.

Jake's keen wits, however, soon read it rightly.

"T' trap's got lost," he said, "and Tom's bin a long time lookin' for un. Come on. We'll soon find him."

Another mile following his tracks and they found another and fresher trail crossing it.

"It's all right, Elsie, lass. That's Tom coming back again. Us needn't follow round. Us'll follow the new track."

The new trail was far from being straight, and at the end of almost half a mile showed evidence of a struggle and a fall.

"Just tripped on his shoes," said Jake; and passed on without stopping.

"Why did he wander about so?" asked Elsie after another period of silence. "Why, he walked right into the tuckamore here!"

"Oh! It was dark, I 'low," answered Jake cheerily. "It's

terrible hard to go straight in the dark. You just shut your eyes and try. The only trouble is, I can't quite make out what's he aiming for. Reckon I'll climb t' knoll while you rests yourself a bit." And without more ado, he started off up the rocky piece of hill. On returning, he said briefly, "T' general line is towards t' green rudge. I thought maybe he'd gone for the tilt there. And anyhow, it's time us cooked a kettle if us wants to keep going."

Though hunger and weariness and self were far enough from Elsie's mind, Jake gave her no time to discuss the proposition, and, having carefully marked where he could, if necessary, strike Tom's trail again, he branched off in the direction of the tilt. Elsie followed for all the world like a child.

Another half-hour passed in silence, and then suddenly Jake, who was ahead, gave a joyous shout.

"Come along, lass," he said. "I thought as much. Here's his trail, and he's surely making for the tilt." "We might have saved the night's wandering," he thought, but was too generous to say so, and merely added, "Tom'll be main surprised to get visitors out here, if so be as he hasn't left again."

Time took wings to itself now, and it only seemed a few moments before the poles marking the track to the tilt, which was hidden in the dense spruces, came into view. Jake, still ahead, went in without waiting, for the marks of the trail had revealed to him a far more anxious tale than he had shown.

Tom was lying face down, stretched out on the big bed of spruce-tips — his arm still round the body of the beautiful silver fox.

A good blazing fire, some hot tea, and dry loaf to eat soon made a difference — and chafing his extremities soon brought back animation to them. He had not been wet and the depth of the soft spruce bed had fortunately afforded him some little heat. Before night the whole three were safely home, and all the village knew that Tom Marvin had caught a silver.

Alas, you can't keep a family on fox-meat and even now that they had good value to exchange for food, it was a serious task to get it. The nearest station was a Hudson's Bay

Company's post, nearly a hundred miles away. Almost all the dogs in the village had either died or been shot, as no one had any food with which to supply them. But all hands were interested, and enough half-fed animals were collected to enable Jake and Tom to set out for the Company's post.

It was two days' journey as a rule with an empty sledge, but it would surely take four days, coming back loaded, with the team available and the chances of bad weather. They hoped to drag back at least three barrels of flour, with fats and other supplies as well, so they were counting on a thousand pounds at the lowest reckoning. That meant the men would have to walk every step of the way back.

As soon as the skin was dried, it was carefully packed, and the two men set out on their journey over mountain valleys and arms of the sea, as light-hearted and confident as schoolboys. They should be back at least a full week before Christmas.

But the appointed time came and went, and still there was no news of the sledge. It was only four days to Christmas when Uncle Joe sent out a relief party on foot, as there were no more dogs left in the settlement.

The children, who had been expecting great things ever since the fox was caught, had been buoyed up on the tiptoe of expectancy with tales of the "wunnerful" Christmas they were going to have.

"No, no; Christmas is Christmas," said Uncle Joe. "I says it do matter. Why, if Santa Claus is to get to Noo Yawk on time, he'm obliged to pass here early. And if that there Jake don't bring un along, I'll 'low he'll never find this here cove t' year."

The growing anxiety of the village was not diminished by the symptoms of still unsatisfied vital organs in the younger members of more than one family. The hope of a happy Christmas for the children had almost been abandoned, when on the morning of Christmas Eve one of the relief party dispatched for the purpose reported the joyful news that the loaded sledge was climbing the last range of hills on the home journey. The enfeebled dogs had been of little or no use. Moreover, half of them had been sacrificed to feed the others. At every uphill the sledge had to be unloaded, and the barrels literally rolled up to the top. Many a time since I have had to laugh as I thought of the two men solemnly starting a kind of egg-and-spoon race, as they pushed their flour barrels up over the long steep hillsides.

But everything has to come to an end, and before sundown the salvo of the last charges of powder in Peace Haven announced the safe return of the expedition. No time was lost in packing and all night was lost in cooking. But, at any rate, Elsie and Jessie and all the other good mothers had something ready for the day of days.

"It seldom rains but it pours," they say — and it seemed so in this case. Late in the evening, while the attention of the village was occupied with their sledge from the north, a noise of shouting and of bells announced the arrival of another team, from the south. Before any one could say a word a great team of Eskimo dogs, with a driver in Eskimo dress and a tall, bearded man in furs, had drawn up at Uncle Joe's door.

"Come right in quick, Doctor," said the old man. "We're just looking for Santa Claus, and I don't know but you's him. Come right in." And in the doctor promptly went, needing, indeed, no second invitation after his long journey.

The plot was soon hatched, Uncle Joe being chief conspirator. "T' box what t' steamer left for you in the fall, Doctor, — I've got it right here. But, of course, there's no knowing what's in un."

"Is it very heavy, Uncle Joe?"

"Well, now, it is and it ain't. I'm thinkin' there's something beyand tinned meat in he."

The box was soon brought in and duly opened. Fortunately I had noticed in Peace Haven, as in many other places on the Labrador, that, beyond cotton reels and other educational but somewhat unsatisfactory substitutes, toys were characterized almost entirely by their absence. Here and there a cheap painted effigy could be seen perched high up on the wall, well out of reach of the children — a precaution probably as salutary for the doll as for the infant. But I had tried to remember this shortage, and before even a tin of milk appeared, a large parcel of toys containing many dolls was discovered.

The midnight round of Santa Claus; the excitement and shouting in the morning; the full meals at which you might eat all you liked, but of course couldn't; the magic lantern slides shown by the doctor in the schoolhouse in the evening — are possibly just so many negligible quantities in the economy of the universe. But they were not in the annals of Peace Haven. Joy filled the heart of Bertie as he clasped to his breast his new calico cat as tightly as had poor Tom the silver fox; bliss reigned in the soul of Johnnie as he strutted from house to house to show his cronies the first Teddy bear that ever braved the climate of our Northland; while to the hearts of Jake and his good wife, of Tom and Elsie, of Uncle Joe and all the grown-ups in the village, not excluding the doctor and the dogs, to whom had been given an extra portion, came the "Salaam" of Him whose Birthday they were keeping, a present which can be given, but never purchased.

"To the Eskimo mind, everything animate or inanimate possesses a soul."

3.
The Northern Lights
Down to the Sea, 1910

As a country for summer holidays, Labrador has not yet been taken seriously. Yet it attracts many scientists who visit it for its unique opportunities for special work. In the summer of 1905, Elihu Root, Secretary of State, came in search of that absolute rest which is impossible in any country where telephones and the other appurtenances of civilization have intruded.

From several points of view, also, Labrador affords attractions offered by no other country so near at hand. The scenery of the southern coast is modified by the fact that in the glacial period the ice-cap smoothed and rounded the mountain peaks, while the cliffs were seldom five hundred feet in height. In the north, however, the mountain tops apparently always reared their heads above the ice stream, and for its high cliffs and virgin peaks and coastline is unrivaled anywhere in the world. The fact that the high land runs right out to the Atlantic seaboard does not prevent its affording most imposing fiords winding away among its fastnesses. For the thundering of the restless Atlantic, the grinding masses of the polar ice, which assail its bulwarks for eight months out of twelve, and the iron frost of its terrible winters, have proved to be workmen that even its adamantine rocks have been unable to withstand.

Thus there have been carved out fiords such as that of Nakvak, which runs inland for thirty miles. The cliffs on each side rise direct from the narrow gorge, which is itself only a mile in width, to an average of about two thousand feet, the deep blue water affording anchorage so close in under the cliffs that one would suppose it bottomless elsewhere. Though these rocks are the basal rocks of the earth's skeleton, and are entirely barren of trees and shrubs — or, indeed, of any fossil either, — their sternness is mitigated by the abundant carpet bedding of brilliant-colored lichens and the numerous small subarctic flora to be found up to their highest peaks. To the north of this inlet are still loftier mountains, the heights of which have not yet been measured, and the summits of which have never yet yielded to the foot of man. A cluster known as the "Four Peaks" has been variously estimated up to six thousand feet in height.

There is no country in the world where the glories of the aurora borealis can so frequently be enjoyed. The weird "northern lights," called by the Eskimo "the spirits of the dead at play," are seen dancing in the sky on almost every clear night. The glorious red morning light, stealing over these rugged peaks, and steeping, in blood, as it were, the pinnacles of the loftiest icebergs in the world, forms a contrast with the deep blue of the ocean and the glistening white in a way that will hold the dullest spellbound. The endless stream of fantastic icebergs at all times enlivens the monotony of a boundless ocean.

Though cruising in north Labrador is at present made difficult by the poor survey of the coast, it is also made delightful to the amateur sailor by the countless natural harbors, never more than a few miles apart, and by the thousands of outlying islands, which permit almost one-fourth of the coast to be visited in perfectly smooth water, the great swell from the Atlantic being shouldered off by the long fringe of them that runs seaward for twenty or thirty miles.

Clearly written in water-worn boulders on the mountain-sides of the now slowly rising land, and by the elevated sea caves, with their wave-washed pillows, is the history of how the Labrador came here. These raise before the dullest mind visions of a paleocrystic sea that lapped these shores in the dim ages of the past. Hanging everywhere on almost imperceptible lodging places on the crests and ridges of every mountain, the ice-carried erratics forever tempt one to climb up and try to dislodge them. But generally one finds they weigh many tons, and this puny strength cannot stir them the single inch necessary to send them crashing down into the valleys below. The Labrador has no towns, no roads, and no policemen. Scattered along its shores one meets, during the months of open water, only the venturous fishing vessels from the far South, manned by their wholesome crews, the stout-hearted vikings of today, and, beside these, the native Eskimo, still almost prehistoric in their customs, and themselves alone of sufficient interest to merit a sideshow at all the recent world's exhibitions. But for the fact that trade and the gospel have gone hand in hand, this "flavor of the past" would have been blotted out long ago. Only around the stations of the brethren of the Moravian Church are there left any number of this interesting people. The good Moravian brethren have acted as traders as well as preachers and teachers. By tabooing liquor and cheap gewgaws, by fair dealing, by the inculcation of simple religion, and by the paternal surveillance of morals, they have almost prevented any decrease in the number of their people in the last fifty years, during which only they have kept a census. Meanwhile the Eskimo have everywhere else virtually vanished from the coast.

This is a tribute to the value of their mission especially unimpeachable, in view of the present-day strenuous efforts to prevent loss of life among children in our crowded cities.

It has not been easy to convey to the Eskimo mind the meaning of the Oriental similes of the Bible. Thus, the Lamb of God had to be translated *kotik*, or "young seal." This animal, with its perfect whiteness as it lies in its cradle of ice, its gentle, helpless nature, and its pathetic, innocent eyes, is probably as apt a substitute, however, as nature offers. Yet not long ago an elderly lady, who at other times had almost a genius for what savored of idolatry, sent me in Labrador a box containing a stuffed lamb, "that the Eskimo," after all these years, "might learn better."

To the Eskimo mind, everything animate or inanimate possesses a soul. Thus, in their graves we found they invariably placed every cherished possession, that their spirits might serve the departed spirit in the same capacities in the life to come. There is little room for burial beneath the scant earth in Labrador, even if the frost would permit it. So the grave consists of upright stones, with long, flat ones laid across. These not only serve to keep the wolves from the body, but wide chinks also afford the spirits free passage in and out.

I have found many graves perched upon some promontory jutting out into the sea, so that the spirit might be near its hunting ground and again take toll from the spirits of departed seals. In a little cache at the foot of the grave are generally to be found the remnants of the man's property. Even since Christianity has come among them, I have seen a modern rifle and good steel snow-knives rusting in the grave; and I have found pipes filled with tobacco, that those who were denied the pleasures of its enjoyment while on earth should at least have a chance given them to learn its use in the regions beyond the grave. No Puritanical forecasts of the joys of heaven trouble the Eskimo mind.

The stone age is only just passing in Labrador. But already the museums of the South are hungering for these witnesses to man's humble origin, and the most easily found graves have been ruthlessly rifled. Indeed, one man came and complained to me that an energetic collector, of unmentionable nationality, had positively carried off the bones of his grandmother! I wished on one occasion to obtain some specimens of stone kettles, axes, knives, and other relics from some ancient graves known to me on a certain island. We had not time, however, to leave our steamer to hunt for them. Out of gratitude for services rendered to them in my capacity as "Aniasuit," or "the man that has to do with pain," some of my little friends readily promised to seek them for me. They explained, however, that they should put something into the grave for each thing they took out. I referred them to the Moravian station, where they could purchase, at my expense, things likely to satisfy the departed spirits, as there was nothing they would have found valuable in my floating drug store.

Now, it so happened that once, when it was the mark of an anarchist in Germany to wear a beard, the German brethren had brought out a job-lot of razors, forgetful that nature had been merciful to the Eskimo in their frigid climes, and spared them superfluous hair about their faces. So the stock was still available, and on returning in the spring I found my friends had solemnly deposited these in the caches they had robbed. The idea of the hoary spirits of their ancestors practising the noble art, in the night watches, on these awful headlands, with inferior razors, appealed to other than the religious sense in us. But the minds of all men are more or less muddled (*teste* Carlyle), and the Eskimo have a singular lack of humor.

As patients, these little people are most excellent. They have no fear of pain, and heal rapidly, a tribute, possibly, to our almost germless air. On one occasion, seated in a large Eskimo *tubik*, or tent, I was seeing the sick of a settlement which I had not visited for eight months. It came the turn of a girl of about fifteen years, who silently held up a frost-bitten toe that needed removing. As there was a dense crowd in the tent, she insisted it should be done at once. The satisfaction of being for the moment the center of attraction was all the anesthetic she wanted.

Gratitude, also, is not so uncommon in Labrador as it was in Judea. I had operated one year, in the North, on a young man with a dislocated shoulder, and had long since forgotten all about him. Some two years later a beaming Eskimo met me

59

at the head of the companion ladder, and produced from beneath his voluminous *kossack* a finely ornamented pair of boots. He soon made clear to me that he had been pursuing me all this time with this token of his gratitude, and kept pointing to the shoulder, which he could now freely use. I have known it otherwise at home with doctors and their fees, where the patient took no unlawful trouble to see his benefactor rewarded.

There are in Labrador settlers and half-breeds who are ever increasing in number, while their pure-blooded brethren are vanishing away. These, too, are an interesting people, retaining many bygone superstitions and customs, some of which they have in common with all fisherfolk. Among these a large part of my practice lies. I append a sample invitation to pay a visit to one of them who was sick. It is an exact copy.

Dr. Docker Greand
Felle Battle Harbor
Labrador.

>Please Docker i sen
>you this to see if
>you call in Sea
>bight when you gose
>down to see Mr. archbell
>Chubbs he in nead
>of you.

A letter like this, however, is a compromise with their own ideas, and to me is the emblem of a better era. For among my first patients, thirteen years ago, on a lonely island, was the father of a budding family. When I called, he was sitting up on his bed, perspiration from pain pouring down his face, and the red lines of a spreading infection running up his arm from a deep poisoned wound in the hand. I showed him that his life was at stake, and that I could painlessly open the deep wound. He absolutely refused, as he had already sent a messenger to an old lady up the bay who was given to "charming." Passing the island again before I left next morning, I found he had not slept since I went away, and the old lady had not yet arrived. He again refused the knife. I did not call again at the island till the following spring, when I was not surprised to find his "tilt" deserted and the roof fallen in. The old lady had not arrived in time, and the neighbors, in their generous way, had shared his children among them.

Having no doctors of their own, they display no small ingenuity in devising remedies from the few resources they possess. Naturally, certain persons are looked upon as specially gifted. The claims of wise women vie with those of seventh sons, but no reasonable person would dispute the priority of the seventh son of a seventh son. "Why, bless yer, worms 'll perish in their open hands." Once, in stripping a fisherman to examine his chest, I perceived that he had a string, as of a scapular, around his neck. Knowing that he was not a Catholic, I asked him the meaning of it. "Sure, 't is a toothache-string, sir," he replied. "Sure, I never had the toothache sunce I worn un." So another, who on one occasion I found to be wearing a green ribbon round his left wrist, told me, " 'T is against the bleedin', sir, if ever I be took."

There are more feet than shoes in many families in Labrador, and we are frequently called upon to amputate legs which have been frozen. Not only do the children suffer from this cause, but men and women as well. I recall a case which proves the unimportance of creed in religion. The wife of a Roman Catholic had a leg amputated, and I was called upon to supply an artificial leg. I had one in stock, and after I had given it to her I learned its history. The leg had been made for a Baptist soldier who lost a limb in the Civil War. When he died, his wife, who was a Presbyterian, kept it for a while and then gave it to an Episcopal cripple. It worked around to my mission in a devious way, and I gave it to the wife of the Roman Catholic.

On one occasion, the burly skipper of a fishing crew boarded the mission ship, his head swathed in red flannel, his cheek blistered with liniment, and his face puffed out like a blue bag.

"Toothache, Skipper Joe?" I said; "you'll soon be all right," and I pulled down a snaky instrument from the row in the charthouse.

"No, no Doctor; I wants un charmed."

"But, you know, I don't charm people, Skipper. Nonsense, I tell you! Get out of the deckhouse!"

But he only stood vociferating on the deck, "No, no, Doctor; 't is only charmin' her wants."

Time is precious when steam is in the boiler, so I merely replied, "Sit on that coaming, and open your mouth."

He waited to see that I had dropped the forceps, and then followed my directions. Waving my hands over his head, I touched the offending molar. His mind seemed greatly relieved, and he at once proffered twenty-five cents for the benefit of the mission. Three months later, on my way south, I saw this man again. Beaming with smiles, he volunteered, "Ne'er an ache nor a pain in 'er since you charmed her, Doctor." While he was showing me the molar, still in its place, to confirm his theory, I was wondering what faith-healing really meant.

On one of my winter journeys with dog team and komatik, we made a long detour to see a sick man. A snow storm overtook us, and we arrived late at night, thoroughly tired out, at the rude tilt where our patient lay. After doing our best for the poor fellow, we stretched out our sleeping bags on the floor preparatory to turning in, as we are in the habit of doing whenever it is desirable to have a private apartment. It was customary for our host's dogs to burrow down through the snow and sleep under the house. For there they got shelter and warmth beneath that part of the floor where the stove stood. Our dogs, having discovered their burrows, desired to share their comforts, but they could not get down to give battle except by crawling down one at a time. The result was a constant growling and barking only a few inches from our heads. Sleep seemed impossible, yet no one wished the task of digging the dogs out.

It so happened that my host's seventh son was at home, and he promptly offered to charm the dogs into quietude. This he did by standing with his back to the wall and apparently twiddling the thumbs of his clasped hands in some peculiar way. He also muttered a few words which he would not tell me. For my part, I was so tired that I went to sleep watching him, and for me, at least, the charm worked. My driver also confessed he thought that it was we who were charmed; for the seventh son had faded from sight and memory while still twiddling his thumbs.

Much more rational than these efforts are some of those in use at sea. The astringent liquor from the boiled scrapings of the hardwood sheave of an old block is no mean remedy when swallowed in quantity; and the boiled gelatinous skin of a flatfish, covered with a piece of an oilskin coat, forms a real rational poultice. "Why, 't will draw yous head to your heels, if you puts her in the right place."

A salt herring, bandaged against the delicate skin of the throat, has much virtue as a counter-irritant; but, like most of these humble remedies, fails in diphtheria, nor saves in the hour of peril some loved child that skilled aid might have rescued.

It is often said that there is no law in Labrador, and I have heard men profane enough to add, "Thank God!" I do not know that the facilities for obtaining satisfactory settlements have evolved in proportion to our sense of justice and the intricacies of our methods of obtaining it. In the capacity of magistrate, I was called on once to settle the division of a property which should have left a small sum to a needy family. I found the cost of division by the usual channels would have left only a zero to divide. So we appealed to equity, and forced one another to abide by it. Only last week a dispute arose about the ownership of a certain plot of land. It had been argued unsuccessfully with high words and with pike-handles. The weaker party applied for a summons. So, appointing the plot of land as the court, and daybreak as the hour, we settled the question between three disputants in exactly fifteen minutes. This included the making of landmarks, which I erected myself. Moreover, the court was able to be back over the hills in time for breakfast, with an excellent appetite and a satisfied mind as his only judicial fees.

There has been no law promulgated as yet in Labrador dealing with the infant mortality and cruelty to children. My first case of this kind involved insistence on a stepfather's assuming the responsibility for a little girl belonging to his new wife. Returning three months later to the same place, I found the man obdurate and the little girl living in a house by herself, where he merely allowed food to be sent to her. There could be no gain to the community by our deporting the man to a prison five hundred miles away in Newfoundland, nor gain to the child by forcing so unnatural a person to allow her to live with him. So the court decided to add the little girl to the crew of his steamer, and steamed away with a new kind of fee. Good, however, came out of evil, for we have since ventured on a small orphanage near one of our hospitals, and I have had the supreme pleasure of taking to its shelter more than one delightful little derelict.

We cannot, however, always be Solomons, and the best-intentioned of decisions may sometimes be at fault. Thus, on one occasion, a man's cow, feeding on the hillside, was found dead in the morning. It had obviously been killed by someone's dogs. As the owner went up to find the body, he saw two dogs coming away suspiciously licking their chops. These belonged to a poor neighbor of his, the guilt of whose team, I fear, was at no time in doubt. He expressed the greatest sorrow, and offered to shoot his dogs. But that would not bring the cow to life again. So, though he had no money, we decided that the cow should be cut in two, each man taking half, the offender to pay half the value of the cow to the owner, in money, as soon as he could. By the valuation of the coast, the cow was worth only twenty dollars. I was alarmed next day to hear that my steward had bought from the aggressor six dollars' worth of meat, and that two other men had bought four dollars' worth, so that the offender was in pocket and distinctly encouraged to kill his neighbor's cow again, especially as his disposition of his half had left him with a fine meal of fresh beef into the bargain.

The uncertainty of a fisherman's calling, and the long winter of forced inaction, when Jack Frost has our hunting grounds in his grip, made the need of some remunerative winter work as necessary to us as a safety valve is to a boiler. We had an excellent belt of spruce and fir trees at the bottom of our long bays, and a number of us agreed to cooperate in a lumber mill, that thus men might be helped to help themselves, rather than be forced to accept doles of free flour and molasses, and at the same time be robbed of their self-respect. So we purchased a boiler engine, and saw table, and the skipper of our coöperative vessel volunteered to bring these weighty impedimenta on his deck from St. John's. I myself was away in the North, beyond the reach of mails, when it suddenly occurred to me that the boiler weighed over three tons, and we had not chosen a spot or built a wharf on which to land it. We had merely applied for an area on which to conduct operations.

But the genius of the sailor saved the situation. For the skipper had found a spot where he could warp his vessel alongside the rocks. He had then cut down some trees, which he had used as skids, and improvising a derrick out of his main and mizzen halyards, he had safely slipped the boiler to the beach. Others had dragged it up on another set of skids, and had built over it a massive mill house, kneed like a capsized schooner, and calculated at a pinch to resist a bombardment. True, we had to bring fresh water a mile and a quarter without pipes, but they had sawed wood enough for this, dammed the river, and carried the troughs on eighteen-foot stakes; and now for several years the mill has been running successfully. We had to learn our trade, and it has cost us much unevenly sawed boarding and at least four fingers, but, beyond that, no serious accidents; and a little winter village has sprung up about this source of work, with a school and a mission room, and we can afford to pay for logs enough to give a winter's diet to one hundred separate families. We have built schooners at the mill, besides other boats, and a lot of building. I am not sure in my own mind which does more to mitigate the many evils that follow in the wake of semi-starvation, our pills or our mill.

The economic conditions of all places largely cut off from communication are, I presume, hampered by the fact that the supplying of the necessaries of life falls into the hands of a monopoly; so that it often happens that the poorer the people are, the higher the prices they have to pay. It is the more galling to those who wish to preach a gospel of help when they discover that these same poor people find it difficult to get market value for their produce.

Here is an illustration of the cash value of independence which I took the other day from the lips of as fine a toiler of the sea as ever trod a quarter-deck. The man has three sons grown up enough to help him in the fishery. After long years as a poor hook-and-line fisherman, living from hand to mouth, the boys made enough money to induce a kindly merchant to build them a schooner on credit. The schooner, named the *Olinda*, cost, ready for sea, with "the bit of food aboard," as she left the narrows of her harbor for the fishery, exactly eighteen hundred dollars. "And us didn't know where us was ever goin' to see it from; and us had three sharemen with us. But us come back, sir, in three months, and sold our catch for twenty-three hundred dollars; so that us had enough to pay our three sharemen, and pay for the schooner, and have one hundred dollars coming to us. Us still had time to go down North again and fetch the freighters us had carried down, and to catch another hundred quintals of fish. The second trip brought us in seven hundred and forty dollars. And now," he said triumphantly, "us is independent, and can buy our bit anywhere us likes; so it will come cheaper, you see, Doctor." It stands to reason every man cannot shake off quite so easily the shackles which bind him to a particular trader.

It was to help others to do what this man was able to do for himself that thirteen years ago we started a series of small coöperative stores. In many cases these have had the effect that we desired.

The reality of a spiritual world is no stumbling block to our people, and indeed all are more or less superstitious as to its relations to the world we now inhabit. Four winters ago an excellent trapper, Joe Michelin, living about twenty-five miles up the magnificent river on which the Grand Falls of Labrador are situated, was in much trouble. His children informed him that they had seen a weird, large, hairy man crossing the little bit of open country between the alders on the river bank and a *drogue* of woods on the other side of his house. A practical-minded man, he put no credence in the story until one day they ran in and told him it had just crossed the open, and they had seen it waving his hands at them from the willows. Rifle in hand, he went out, and to his intense surprise found fresh, strange tracks in the direction in which the children had told him the creature had gone. These marks sank into the ground at least six inches, where the horses that work at the mill would only have sunk two inches. The mark of the hoof was distinctly cloven, and the strides were at times no less than eight feet apart.

Knowing that he would not be credited if he told this story even to his nearest neighbor, who lived some miles away, he boarded over some of the tracks to preserve them from the weather. At night time his dogs would often be growling and uneasy, and several times he found they had all been driven into the river during the night. He himself heard the monster walking around the house in the dark, and twice distinctly heard it tapping on the downstairs shutter. He and his family were so thoroughly frightened that they always slept in the top loft of their house, with loaded revolvers and rifles beside them.

The tracks became more numerous as the spring opened, and one day his boy of fourteen told him that he, too, had seen the creature vanishing into the trees. A French-Canadian trapper, hearing of his trouble, came over to see the tracks, and was so impressed that he hauled over four bear traps and set them in the paths. Michelin himself would sit day after day at the window, his repeating rifle in his hand, and not leaving his position even for meals, on the off chance of a shot at his unearthly visitor. The chief wood ranger from the big mill told me he had seen the tracks but what to say of them he did not know. No new tracks appeared for some weeks, however, and Michelin quite recovered his equanimity.

The insistence on dogma has found little place on the program of the workers of our Labrador Mission. Our efforts to interpret the message we would convey are aimed rather in the direction of endeavoring to do for our fellow men on this coast, in every relation of life, those things which we should like them to do for us in similar circumstances.

As I sit writing in the charthouse, I can read across the front of the little hospital off which we are anchored the words of a text thirty-six feet long. It was carved in solid wood by the boys' class in Boston. It reads: "Inasmuch as ye have done it unto one of the least of these my brethren, ye have done it unto me."

I have most faith in unwritten sermons. Still, the essential elements of our faith are preached orally at times by all of us. And in this relation it has been my good fortune at times to have a cook or a deckhand equally able with myself to gather a crowd on a Sunday morning to seek God's blessing on these barren rocks. We can also believe that the noble amphitheaters that these mighty cliffs afford us are as likely to prove "Bethels" as were ever the more stately erections of the genius of man. I have seen new men made out of old ones on this very coast, new hopes engendered in the wrecks of humanity. So that once, when whispering into the ear of a dying man on board a tiny schooner, and asking him if the years since the change took place in him had been testified to by his life, in the most natural way in the world he was able to answer, "I wish you'd ask my skipper, Doctor." We have seen in our tiny hospitals the blind made to see, the lame made to walk, and the weak and fearful strengthened to face the Valley of the Shadow of Death. But the object of the Labrador Mission is to help men to live, and not to die; and so to live as not merely to cumber this earth for a few more years, but to live as worthier sons of that great Father whose face we all expect one day to see.

Grenfell in the men's ward of his hospital at St. Anthony.
"The tax on our nervous energies had been a fact."

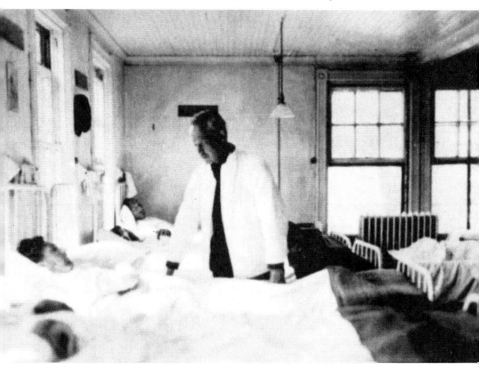

4.
Remedy for Worry
Down North on the Labrador, 1910

Cut off by the frozen sea for the long winter months as a general rule, we enjoy the enforced simple life, and store up energy for the open season. But last year it had been a very wearing time with us at the hospital.

It was not because our patients had not done well; on the contrary, we had had more reason than enough to be satisfied with our results.

Beyond letters of gratitude from those to whom still a modern surgical operation is a miracle, and who are also tender-hearted enough to express their feelings, each successive mail-steamer had brought us an increasing number of sufferers ever coming from longer distances, whom it was our enlarging privilege to help.

The comparatively small fall of snow had made some of our longer journeys by dogsledge physically exacting, which in our experience is as a rule the best antidote for worry of mind. It had added, however, its quota to a strenuous time, and the tax on our nervous energies had been a fact even if we had not recognized it.

On the top of this there had been financial worries; the doubling of the hospital had increased the running expenses greatly; the enlargement of the orphanage meant a further increase in upkeep.

We had discovered that the new school, simply essential if we were to be able to give the "whole man" the uplift needed, could not be built for the money donated.

My colleague looking after the new sailors' home had written that the contract was much larger than he had expected or could afford.

The poor price for fish, with a very moderate fishery, had made it very hard times with some of our poor friends and neighbours along the shore.

The "coöperative" or people's stores that we had started and been fostering were wondering whether they could meet their liabilities.

On account of lack of communication we were powerless to prevent some plans from being carried out that from experience, gained recently, we now knew would involve probably considerable loss and suffering.

Everything seemed to come at once, and we were caged in and powerless to do anything to remedy things.

The seat of the human emotions is a physical thing, and even to the optimist the world will look blue when nervous vitality is exhausted.

Though it certainly goes hard with me to confess, it was in just such a mood that I was sitting watching our mission boat, which some friends had collected the money for, and which seemed only able to say to me, "Ought you to go to the expense of my upkeep, when there is more than enough work coming to you anyhow?"

Its beautiful lines and costly outfit rendered it a perfect handmaid to our work; but to my distorted view, as I was worrying over the unkind comments of an enemy, who had been accusing a missionary of being self-indulgent, even his helpmate was out of joint.

The ice had gone now; but open water with all its undoubted blessings had brought us an incessant stream of poor folk coming for sympathy and help, and also an endless delayed correspondence and a complexity of problems that permitted little relief from nervous strain.

Every man's lot seemed to be better than my own; and, as the white-winged fleet flitted north in quest of its harvest of the sea, the cheering welcome of our many passing friends seemed only to emphasize my own troubles.

My introspective mood was, however, abruptly interrupted by a maid announcing, "There are some men to see you, doctor; they seems in a terrible hurry."

In the waiting-room I found six broad-chested, blue-jerseyed vikings, who had rowed over from their island home twenty miles away to the southward.

With characteristic bluntness only a vise-like grip of the hand preceded the announcement of their business, which was that Paddy Dunster's wife had "borned her eighth baby ten days ago," but had "got the fever," and was very near to dying. Would I go over at once?

Our mail-steamer only twenty-four hours previously had landed forty-nine sick folk at our door, and we had not only a large group of surgical operations ahead of us, but some few patients already fresh from the operating room.

Even while my colleague and I were debating the possibilities of going, another lot of men were reported by the maid, and they also were "terrible anxious."

This time in the hallway I found almost a replica of the first group, and immediately recognized them as coming from about ten miles to the north.

"Elisha Marston's woman is very sick and like to die. Her baby was borned two days ago, and there were no one to see to her. We wants you to come right along at once. Us 'll carry you back glad enough."

It wasn't an easy matter to decide, but it was somewhat the stimulus I needed; namely, the realization that there was a need for what one had to give.

While I was still undecided as to what to do, my eye fell

inadvertently on the missionboat at the wharf.

Oddly enough, it upbraided me no longer. Instead it said perfectly plainly, "Come at once, and I'll take care of you." What more was needed?

A few hours later, as happy as a cricket at the prospect of the trip, I was chasing the already departed trap-boat, which had disappeared at a pace that I have seen exhibited only in boats rowed by just these men, and by them only when they are bound on sick-calls.

Meanwhile, my colleague, having satisfied himself that the condition of the "in" patients permitted it, left to answer the northward call, and, preferring shank's pony over the hills to the longer route by water, was toiling already through tuckermore and over bog, through brooks and over rocks and barrens, for no fee but a woman's life.

As we drew towards the island, a second hurrying boat met us. The helmsman waving his hands caused us to stop, when he boarded us with a letter from our poor patient's husband.

It ran:

> *Dear Doctor:* I knows you'se coming; but Mary's no better, and it's five o'clock, and there's no signs of you. Do come along quick, doctor. I knows you will.
>
> PATRICK DUNSTER.

Without a word except of greeting on landing I was hurried right into the sick-room.

It needed no special insight to recognize the danger. The collapsed condition of my patient, and the flickering pulse, showed that if there was any hope of recovery at all, it lay in immediate action.

It was already dark, and the house I had come to was very small. The other seven children were only too obviously at home, while the baby and its attendants occupied, to say the least, all the room that could be spared them.

Cold is still supposed to be harmful by our people. Heat is

man's friend. Therefore the windows were closed, and the stove was in full blast.

I had served a long apprenticeship in these troubles, and have learned that a people accustomed to one ritual do not resent another, and also that a little trouble can transform even such an environment into a possible room for effective surgery. Without delay the transformation was accomplished and the last chance given.

Every time the door was open Pat's eager face asked, even before the words came, "How is it going with Mary?"

By ten o'clock all was quiet again, and every effort was being made to keep life in my patient till she should reap full benefit of the work.

At midnight in spite of all precautions there were no signs of rallying; the balance of the scales seemed to hang by a hair.

One o'clock passed safely; two struck; and still there was hope.

But it was now, alas! only the hope of a David in the anguish that made him exclaim, "Who can tell whether God will be gracious to me, that the child may live?" The battle was going against us, and my tired brain seemed unable to afford any further suggestions.

I tried to explain it to my poor friend, but the intuition of love had already revealed to him the probable outcome.

While there was still hope, yet there was nothing further I could do. Other duties would be pressing on us with the returning day; so I gladly accepted the kindly suggestion that I should lie down to await events.

It hardly seemed five minutes later when my opening eyes fell on the figure of Pat standing by the couch.

Daylight was breaking, and the infinite loneliness and silent sorrow in his face made any questions unnecessary. He had come to tell me that I had lost.

It was a perfect morning that was breaking outside; not a ripple could be seen on the placid waters of the Atlantic. Only now and again the flash of an oar or the bumping of a boat

75

against a schooner's side broke the silence, and reminded us that the world must go on in spite of our sorrow.

The lack of wind to carry us on our homeward journey gave us time to linger, while the last sad offices that could be rendered to the poor wife and mother were willingly performed by kindly hands.

It would be a time that in many homes would make any attempt at offering comfort seem an intrusion. But here in the face of the immediate sad outlook for this large family of small children an excuse was furnished us for not hastening away, and an opportunity was opened for assuring our old friend of so many years that he might count on us to stand by him, without appearing to trespass on his grief.

Years ago his right hand had been shot to pieces by an explosion of his gun while the hand rested on the mussle as he loaded the other barrel. It had been my privilege then to be able, after many weeks of constant attention, not only to save his life, but to patch up the fragments left sufficiently to enable him to nip a fishing line while he hauled it in with the other hand, and thus follow his calling successfully.

It had ever since been a very close bond of affection between us. It gave me a privilege that with complete strangers in the hour of distress I should have hesitated to exercise; so that, when at last we started homewards in the boat, we had the small comfort in the consciousness of our failure that we could still be of service.

Moreover, we also had the welcome assurance that confidence in our ability to serve had not been shaken; for among the friends present was waiting a young mother with her only child, a babe of fifteen months, to accompany me back to the hospital for a dangerous operation on the brain. This has since been successfully performed.

As I reached the hospital and began storing away in their places the various apparatus that we had chosen to rely on for help in our unequal task, the nurse informed me that my colleague had just returned also, and was now seeking a well-earned rest upstairs. Success had crowned his efforts; and, as I peeped into his room, I could see he was enjoying the restful repose of the victor.

To many it would seem that the personal unrest in which this call to service had found me must have been enhanced by this additional exaction. To my surprise it proved absolutely the reverse. A few hours later I awoke to realize the fact that I had enjoyed the most refreshing sleep for many months.

The mission-boat was still at her old place at the wharf when I looked out of the window.

There was no upbraiding about her this time. She just said: "Capacity is worth paying for. Here I am waiting again."

On the hill behind her stood the enlarged hospital, and the long row of patients sunning themselves on the veranda and upstairs balcony seemed all to say, "We may have cost money, but we pay you in opportunity and a full life."

Further back stood the orphanage; a batch of hatless, barelegged children as happy as sandhoppers were skipping around outside, waiting to accompany the schoolma'am to school. They seemed to say, "God will provide for us; and you have no right to worry."

On the other side of the hilltop rose the spire of our little church. It had an odd message this morning, in which it seemed at first to be stultifying itself, for it said plainly so that I could not but understand: "I cannot give you peace. Not in creed or sect can you find it. Kindness is more Christlike than righteousness. His peace comes only to those travelling in His footsteps. The remedy for unrest is work."

'Tis something, when the day draws to its close,
To say, 'Though I have borne a burdened mind,
Have tasted neither pleasure nor repose,
Yet this remains: to all men, friends or foes,
    I have been kind.'
                                    — DAWSON

Grenfell at the ship's wheel. "There was that in the womb of the future which at that time they little reckoned of."

5.
Rescue at Sea
Down to the Sea, 1910

The good fore and aft schooner *Rippling Wave* had made a most successful run to her market, which happened this year to be in the Mediterranean. The fact that she had not left the Labrador coast till late in October was no fault of hers or the skipper's; for if there was one ocean-going skipper on the coast known to be more of a "snapper" than the rest, that man was Elijah Anderson. If all the tales were true, Old 'Lige had been known to clap on his topsails when other men were lacing their reef earrings.

Ordered to Patras in Greece, the *Rippling Wave* had out-distanced several rivals who started before her from Labrador, and had "caught the market on the hop" — fish was scarce and therefore in such demand that her cargo fetched splendid prices.

When at last she started on the return journey to her Newfoundland home, after calling to Cadiz for a cargo of salt, no lighter-hearted, happier bunch of men ever trod a good ship's deck. The fact that it was the first day of December didn't cause them even to look at the weather glass, or think of anything but the stories they would be telling of their great good fortune alongside their own firesides by Christmas Day.

But man proposes and God disposes, and there was that in the womb of the future for the crew of the *Rippling Wave* which at that time they little reckoned of. By the middle of the month they were only in 40⁰ west longitude and 40⁰ north latitude. This did not distress her skipper — though if he would make sure now of being at home by Christmas Day, he could not afford to ease the ship down for a trifle.

The third Friday was a dirty day. The barometer was unaccountably low, and the heavy head sea made pressing even the *Rippling Wave* to windward in the dark somewhat dangerous to the hands on deck. As the Mate went on deck for the night watch, the Skipper remarked half apologetically to him as he was putting on his oilskins, "You can heave her to till daylight, Jim, if you thinks well."

After one or two seas, more curly than usual, had rolled on deck, Jim did "think well," and till midnight the hands below enjoyed the leisurely motion that these handy vessels assume when jogging "head to it" in a long sea.

Skipper 'Lige had just turned in when he felt something touch him on the arm. He started up, to find a figure in dripping oilskins bending over him.

The Mate wanted him on deck to give an opinion as to a strange darkness that seemed to be crossing the ship's path low down over the water. Half a second was enough for him to get his head out of the hatchway, following the Mate who had scurried up before him, and his experience at once told him the truth. "Jump for your life, Jim!" he yelled; "it's a water spout." The two men had hardly time to fall in a heap down the companion ladder, when something struck the good ship like a mighty explosion.

Over she went — shook — trembled — rose again; and then up — up — up went the cabin floor, both men being hurled against the for'ard bulkhead, which temporarily assumed the position the floor had occupied the moment before. The *Rippling Wave* was standing literally on her head, and it was a question which way she would come down.

But there wasn't time to get anxious about it. Another mighty heave or two, a sudden sickening feeling, and the two men were rolling about in the water on the cabin floor. But the ship was evidently the right way up. "On deck!" roared the Captain, and both men were up in time to know that the crew, who had been literally drowned out for'ard, were also scrambling aft in the darkness to learn what to do next. All lights were out, and everything was awash.

They soon realized that virtually everything for'ard had gone by the board; for the solid spout water had hit the foremast about half way up, and had then broken, falling in countless tons on the devoted deck. For'ard of the middle line nothing was left. The mast, boom, gaff and sails were missing, with rigging, ropes and everything attached. The bowsprit, jibboom, winch and paulbitts, anchors, chains, fore-companion, fore-hatch and galley were nowhere to be seen. The decks were torn open so widely that one man fell through to his thigh between two strips of planking. Much of the bulwarks and stanchions were gone, as were also both the lifeboats and jollyboat. Every drop of water that came aboard poured into the hull, threatening to engulf the ship in a few minutes. Probably what saved her was the fact that some of the torn remnants of canvas were still on deck, or rather in it, for the last of the fore-staysail was so hard driven through the open seams above the foc'sle, that the men were unable to start a rag of it.

With the doggedness that characterizes such men, they had succeeded before daylight in getting out of the waterlogged cabins some nails and spare canvas, and with these they had covered over every large opening. Below the water line the solid-timbered vessel was still apparently sound, though the stump of the foremast was unstepped, with the result that its foot, rolling round in the deck gammon, was so thumping the bilge inside that it threatened every moment to smash through the sides. There was enough left of it, however, above decks, to make it valuable for a "jury-mast," and the Mate with two volunteers climbed down into the hold and succeeded in jamming it into an upright position.

The rest of the crew stood to the pumps. Daylight, struggling through the murky sky, revealed a situation that looked hopeless enough.

For forty-eight hours every man was at work helping to jettison the salt and every other available ounce of weight that could be dispensed with, or taking his trick at the pumps, under the stern eye and unflinching example of Skipper 'Lige.

Hour after hour, without a wink of sleep or any refreshment but pieces of hard biscuit that once had been dry, they fought on with sullen strength and energy.

At last the instinct of self-preservation began to lose its energy, as there came time to think, and they began to realize the apparent futility of continuing the unequal struggle.

It must be remembered that it was the dead of winter. They were in the middle of the North Atlantic. The water was bitterly cold, and they were bruised, wet and exhausted. They were, too, far out of the winter route of trans-Atlantic liners. The chance of being picked up seemed infinitesimal, and it was obvious that with no boat left it was impossible to escape from the wreck.

They were apparently making no headway in raising the ship out of the water. They were merely keeping her afloat. But if 'Lige Anderson were to abandon hope it meant abandoning himself, and he was still sane. In the hours between the spells of the pumping, which he shared with his men — hours which he ought to have devoted to rest, — the Skipper had by no means been idle, and he was now able to hearten the rest with three discoveries he had made.

First, the after half of the ship was absolutely sound; so were her mainmast and sails. Moreover, he had been able to rig a "jury" — rudder, which more or less guided the ship. He had set to work with these as a basis to rig a jury-foremast that would carry a small sail.

Secondly, he had found his logbook and sextant, and

though the latter proved useless owing to the sun being continually invisible, it certainly was a source of hope. The last entry in the logbook on the day before the accident led him to the conclusion that he was about fifty miles south of the track of the ocean liners.

Thirdly, from his almanac he found that there was still a forlorn chance that some steamers might still be running by the northern route.

It was difficult to make sure which way the wreck was really moving. But he could now keep her heading somehow to the west'ard, and it was possible that she might still be worked to a position where they could expect to be sighted if such was the case. A more trivial discovery, but one that counted not a little in the hearts of his Newfoundland crew, was an old tin paintpot, with a sound bottom. This Captain 'Lige had managed to clean up, and over the tiny stove in his cabin he had been able to brew enough hot tea to serve out a drink all round. Heartened by the warm tea, they stood to the pumps again, as night came on, with fresh faith and energy. If only they could make a hundred miles of northing their lives might yet be spared.

A week had now gone by since the accident, and a settled gloom, close akin to despair, had settled upon the men. Then, just in the nick of time, the sun for the first time shot out thro' the drift about midday, and the Skipper was able to get his bearings and tell them that, though they were farther to the westward, they had made at least thirty miles to the nor'ard also. Moreover, he was wise enough, seeing that they were rather more than holding their own, to tell off one man from each watch to keep a lookout from the mainmast head. Though nothing was seen to encourage them, yet the fact that the Skipper believed it was now likely that they would sight something, acted as a fresh charm, and for yet another four days the *clank, clank, clank* of the pumps maintained its even tenor.

By the fifteenth morning all faith in the possibility of

salvation had so departed from some of the men, that they formally proposed to give up striving, and that all hands should go to the bottom together. Skipper 'Lige was at his wits' end. Violence was out of the question. His only subterfuge was in continually pointing his sextant at the lowering clouds, in inscribing endless successions of figures in his books, and at last in announcing that he had discovered they had reached their desired goal. Having called them together, he pointed out to them on his well-thumbed chart, that they now lay exactly on the 49th parallel of latitude. A great cross that he had made on it signified the position of the ship. Exactly through this point ran many lines stretching from the Fastnet to New York, intersecting in his picture the spot that represented the ship. "Them there lines," he announced, "be the tracks o' them big steamers. They always races across, and this be the shortest way for 'em to go."

It would not have required much acumen on the part of the audience to detect the fact that the lines on the paper were not as old as the discourse suggested. But men in the condition of these poor fellows are not inclined to be critical. All that was required of them was to move a handle up and down, and the Skipper had staked his all on their not questioning what he told them. They scanned his face narrowly, and saw that he seemed so hopeful that once again the poor fellows returned to their duty at the pumps.

The morning of the seventeenth day broke with a clear horizon under an oily, sullen sky. The remnant of a ship still tossed up and down, up and down, on the troubled waters. Forward the *Rippling Wave* looked now only like a bunch of weather-beaten boards. Hour by hour, the weary clank of the pumps alone announced that there was any life aboard, and that she was more than a mere derelict on that dreary expanse of waters.

It was 10:00 a.m. when the watch at the masthead called the Skipper. "Smoke on the horizon to the east-northeast," he shouted. So far gone were some of the men that they took no notice of the announcement; even if they heard, it seemed too wonderful to be true. But in two seconds the Skipper was aloft by the side of the watch, and shouting "Steamer coming, boys; keep her going!"

Little by little the cloud, at first no larger than a man's hand, grew bigger and bigger, till the hull of a vessel was visible like a tiny speck beneath it.

The excitement on board can better be imagined than described. But though their eyes were strained to the utmost, they could not make out that the stranger got the least bit nearer, and it wasn't long before 'Lige realized that no help could be expected from that quarter. For the speck grew no larger, and eventually disappeared again behind the wilderness of waters.

The reaction was proportionate to the exhilaration, and an awful despondency fell upon all hands when their hope of safety had again sunk out of sight.

The Skipper's resourcefulness was not exhausted, however, and he spoke to the crew as if he were in the greatest spirits. "You see we'll be all right now, boys," he said. "Our reckoning be just as I told you. Us'll work a mile or two more to the nor'ard, and be home by the New Year if we aren't by Christmas." He took care to emphasize his faith by serving out an extra and earlier dinner, so that, in spite of themselves, not a man slackened at the pumps, and the everlasting clank droned monotonously on.

The afternoon was wearing away, when suddenly once again the eagle eye at the masthead spied smoke. This time it was in the western sky and 'Lige took a bigger risk. Inside planking was torn from the sides of the hold to make a bonfire. So big grew the pile that it could scarcely be kindled without endangering the vessel. As the speck grew bigger, hope grew proportionately large, and without any word from the Skipper, the pulse rate of the pump reached a fever speed. Closer and closer came the stranger. It seemed impossible that she should pass now without seeing them. Evidently she was a small cargo tramp in ballast, and no doubt lightly manned. She was now almost abeam, but still she showed no signs of recognition. 'Lige, through his glasses, learned that there was no one on the upper bridge. That she was an endless time approaching seemed to him their best chance of being seen. For surely *someone* would be on deck to sight them before it was too late. But she passed them by like a phantom ship with a crew of dead men on board; and to this day no one on board knows why.

It was getting dark, and the wind was rising again, with a sea making from the nor'west. The suspense as the steamer passed by had made the enfeebled men conscious of the bitterness of death, and aroused in them an emotion that was perilously near to fear.

There could be no disguising the fact that the end was very near at hand. The mere pretense of work that they were now able to make was at last permitting the water to gain on the pumps; and finally the relief watch failed to stand to their work. There seemed to be no hope. The night promised to be their last on earth.

The horizon had already faded into the lowering sky overhead, and before the sun rose again, the long-drawn agony would be over, and the bitterness of death passed.

But it was not to be. Suddenly a loud cry rang from for'ard. Sure enough, there was a bright light away to the eastward, now and again bobbing up over the waters. It has always seemed right to Skipper 'Lige that their salvation should have come out of the East.

It was plain to him that his last move in the game of life must now be played. He was always known as a silent man, but on this occasion a corpse would have heard him. He had but recently come down from the main masthead, where he had been fixing fast to the crosstrees a barrel full of combustibles. Now, forcing an unlighted flare into the hands of the Mate, "To the masthead," he roared, "and light up when I do! Up the foremast!" he screamed into the ear of his third hand, above the roaring of the wind and sea, "and take this old can o' tar with yer." For'ard and aft he led the rest with their axes. All were working like madmen, with a strength that was like the final flareup of a flickering lamp. Soon large pieces of wood had been torn off from the hatches, lockers, rails, bulwarks, and even the decking. They hacked it from anywhere, so long only as the pile on deck should grow in size. But even as they worked the water was steadily increasing in the hold, and every man was conscious that the *Rippling Wave* was sinking under them.

Sometimes — it seemed for ages — the approaching light disappeared from view; yet the axes kept going, and the pile of wood steadily grew. To restrain the crew from setting fire to it during these interminable intervals required a nerve on the part of the Skipper that they themselves no longer possessed. But even at that moment, with death standing at their very side, they were held to an absolute obedience. Their reverence for their indomitable Captain had long since grown into a superstitious fear. As it was, the sound of axe and lever, as once on the walls of ancient Rome, alone broke the death-like silence every man maintained.

Suddenly, without a moment's warning, a huge black mass rose up out of the water, towering far overhead like some fabulous monster of the sea. The right moment had arrived. So 'Lige Anderson fired his last shot, and lit his flare. In an instant the vessel was ablaze. Fore and aft, aloft, and on the water line, the ship seemed one roaring mass of flames, which shot high into the heavens above her each time the waterlogged hull rolled heavily to windward. A moment later a brilliant search light still further blinded the men on her deck, and afforded the pleasure-seekers who were crowding to the rail of that floating palace (for it proved to be a steamer on a trip round the world) such a scene as in their lives they are never likely to look on again.

The huge steamer turned to wind'ard and stopped short close to them. A loud voice called through a megaphone, "Can you hold on till morning?" There was no hesitation in giving, and no possibility of doubting, the answer. "No, we are sinking!" called Skipper 'Lige. "We are played out; we can't last till daylight."

Words are poor things at best, but the words that came back this time thrilled them all as words had never thrilled before. "Then stand by; we'll try for you now." The Captain on the bridge had no need to ask for volunteers, though the night was black as pitch by now, and the danger of launching a boat in that rolling sea was a terrible one indeed.

There was no lack of skill, no undue haste, no shortage of tackle as a lifeboat was lowered from the side. But long ere the boat had reached the water, a heavy sea had swung her into the iron wall of the ship's side and smashed her to fragments. Those on the wreck had witnessed the attempt, and also the failure, and the ominous swash of the water in the hold seemed louder and more threatening than a few minutes ago.

The big ship had forged ahead. By the time she had regained her position, a wooden lifeboat was already on its way down from the davits with the men in it. Every movement was visible from the *Rippling Wave* as the lifeboat reached the water. The port oars were out, but before the for'ard tackle was free, a great sea drove her into the vessel's side again. The rescuing party were themselves with difficulty rescued. Their boat was a bundle of matchwood.

All eyes were fixed on the steamer. Could it be possible that they would be discouraged and give up? Even Skipper 'Lige expected to be hailed again, and warned that he *must* keep afloat till daylight. But the men on the liner were real sailors, and not the faintest idea of abandoning the attempt ever entered their heads.

The only question with the Captain was, which boat next; as if it were a simple question of which tool would best serve to complete a job that had to be done. A light, collapsible lifeboat seemed to promise most. While the ship was again getting into position, this was made ready. The men took their places in her and were almost literally dropped over the side, as the monstrous ship lurched heavily to wind'ard. There was just one moment of doubt, and then arms and shoulders that knew no denial shot their frail craft clear of the ponderous iron wall. Scarcely a moment too soon did they reach the *Rippling Wave.* Her decks were little better than awash, when Skipper 'Lige, the last man to leave, tumbled over the rail into the lifeboat. Even his dog had preceded him.

Nor was the wreck left to be a possible waterlogged derelict, to the danger of other ships. What was left of the kerosene oil was poured over her as a parting unction and then fired. Before the last man was safe aboard the steamer, however, the *Rippling Wave,* mantled like Elijah's chariot in "flames of fire," had paid her last tribute to the powers she had so long successfully withstood.

A line fastened to a keg having been thrown over from the steamer's side, was picked up without approaching too near. With that absence of hurry that characterizes real courage, the lifeboat kept off (with her stern to the dangerous side of iron) until each of the rescued men had been safely hauled aboard in breeches of cloth, secured to a running tackle. Even the dog would have been saved in the same way, had he not with vain struggling worked loose from the breeches and fallen into the sea; as it was, before getting the lifeboat aboard, the Captain was humane enough to peer round everywhere with his searchlight, in the hope of finding it. The rescued were stripped, bathed and fed, and snugly stowed in beds such as they had seldom even seen before.

From the kindly passengers, more new and warm clothing poured in upon them, next day, than they had ever dreamed of possessing, and the journey to land was as remarkable to them for its luxuries as had been the past fortnight for its privations.

Though Christmas Day had after all been spent on the *Rippling Wave,* New Year's eve found them in the lap of luxury. At dinner in the grand saloon, to which every man was invited, Skipper 'Lige occupied the seat of honor next the

Captain. There was a general feeling that it was a great occasion. Never before had the close of an old year spoken so forcibly of the fickleness of life to many of the others present. After a few seasonable and brief speeches had been made by some of the guests, the climax was reached when the Captain — who, at his own expense, had ordered some dozens of champagne to be served out all 'round — in terse sailor language proposed the toast of the evening. There were few dry eyes among those who drank "To the wives and children of the brave men it has been our good fortune to save."

Grenfell poses with others on ship.

Dr. Grenfell visits a sick fisherman in his bunk. "On the verge of a long Labrador winter, from the thread bare cottage of a defenseless woman and a dying man, I was carrying all their material wealth."

6.
The Gifts of Poverty
Tales of the Labrador, 1916

The annual exodus from Labrador which characterizes the approach of winter had begun, as some willow grouse, in their exquisite fall plumage, and a brace of fine fat geese hanging in our rigging testified.

On every hand it was written that Dame Nature was busy with her winter preparations. She had posted her order to us to "get out quick," in brilliant and insistent letters of salt-water ice on our freeboard. She had added a glittering, new, white "Plimsoll mark" right round our water-line, and had attached large white travelling tags to the links of our anchor chain. The whirring wings of large companies of sea birds, "southward-bound," kept sounding a curfew to us to follow. Even our codfish were forsaking the shallows, and seeking the deeper and darker waters at the word of Her-who-must-be-obeyed. The mate, sitting on the rail, had apparently been reading my thoughts, for he suddenly broke in, " 'Tis getting on time, Doctor, to be thinkin' of them poor underwriters, ain't it?"

A little later, if a landlubber had not noticed the square blue flag with its white center at our masthead, he would have wondered what gave such spring to the heels of our sailors, who, to look at, were far from being fairies.

A ship half the size of Columbus's, the Atlantic still farther north and grown no more docile with age, the winter equinox past, long nights, heavy winds, and high seas expected, not a little forbidding ice dotted about the horizon — all these together cannot stop men who have a vision of home from whistling at their work. Indeed, the only additional tonic to be desired by a healthy soul was just a good, keen problem.

At these times the responsive nature of our men of the sea simply overflows with kindness. A company of our Labrador friends, warned of our departure by the blue peter at our main, had swarmed aboard to bid us "au revoir." Yet, in spite of all, and of many little souvenirs which we saw passing from our seamen's kit bags to those of their friends, to whom even such small gifts were of no mean value, an air of gloom hung over the section of the little world on deck — a tinge of the sorrow which eternally hangs over things human and transient.

Among the group on deck we found two of our oldest friends. They were of a more reserved type than a lonely environment usually produces, but they were known as bosom companions, first-class workmen, and excellent neighbors in time of need. When we wished a hospital completed, when one of our boats had been injured and needed repairing, — indeed, whenever any difficulty overtook any one, — it was always to Uncle Ben and Uncle Abe that our little world turned; and when it did so, it never found them wanting.

We knew that all our friends were suffering from a particularly poor fishing season, and we who were bound for home and plenty could not but feel a soft spot for those left to face what might turn out to be the hard hand of hunger.

"Are you going to meet your debts and have anything coming to you this winter, Uncle Abe?" I queried.

"When my father died, Doctor," he replied, "he left me in debt to the traders. I just turns in all I gets — they knows I do — so they keeps me along. But it will be a bit hard this time, I knows. You can't expect them to feed folks for nothin'. There won't be no luxuries, I'm 'lowing," he laughed.

"That was a bad heritage. I should hate to leave it to any son of mine."

"Bad enough, Doctor, but I'm gettin' on in life, and the Lord hasn't given us ne'er a child — and" — he turned his head away, as he said it, though I knew of what he was thinking — "well, something may come along yet."

It is hard that the necessities of one's life should depend on the whim of another, and that the dreadful cloud of want should hang over the old age of men, who, at great risk to life and with hard labor, have spent all their active years toiling as producers for their country.

Now, years after the event told in this story, an old-age pension has been granted them.

There were tears on Uncle Abe's weather-beaten cheeks as he turned round again. They were not for himself, but I knew it was of the beloved partner of his life that he was thinking.

"How about you, Uncle Ben? They tell me you have been meeting some head winds these past two years."

"There was never a truer word, Doctor. What wi' losin' nets in the ice last fall, and then t' schooner on Deadman's Rocks this spring, there won't be much left to fill the breadbox, come settlin' day."

"Oh, I'm sure the trader will do as well by you as by Uncle Abe," I answered. "Only yesterday he was telling me you were the best dealer he had. He said you had never been in debt yet."

"Maybe he would, and maybe he wouldn't," was the reply. "But I've never owed a man a cent yet, and it will be a dry diet for us before I gets into any man's hands."

"You don't mean that you were born and bred in Labrador, and were never in debt?"

"That's what I does, Doctor. I settles accounts every October-end those forty years since I fended for myself, and the Lord's been that good to me that I've come out square every time. Yes, and had enough not to be hungry either, thank God," he said fervently.

"I don't know many other men on the coast who could say

that, Uncle Ben."

"Maybe there aren't many, but there aren't many like my Mary, either. She's been better than another half of any voyage I ever made. If she hadn't, there'd have been many a hungry mouth beyond mine, when them who is run out has to take to the komatik trail for a meal in winter. Why, she found something for every soul of twenty-odd folk what brought up for a week at our house one time this spring, and over fifty dogs ate what they left behind them."

When I thought of his meager stock, it sounded like the old story of the widow's cruse, only here it was the woman who was the "window from heaven." If I had to guess, I should say that that widow of Sarepta was from Labrador, for her heart, like those in Labrador, was so much larger than her pocket.

Before sailing we slipped ashore, and the merchant's agent kindly let me see the books, which loom up like the one mentioned in Revelation, to our imagination in Labrador. It was all true — Uncle Ben had never once failed to meet his score; and moreover, there was a real chance to give Uncle Abe a hand. Both families "tided out" that winter.

Ten years slipped away. We had sold our little sailing hospital boat, and in the steamer which replaced her were running into the same harbor near Capelin Cove. Suddenly a flag floating at half-mast on the hilltop caught my eye.

"What's wrong ashore?" I shouted to a group of men hauling a herring-net which lay almost in the fairway.

"Uncle Abe's missus be gone. They're burying her tonight."

An hour later, sorrowful enough at heart for my poor friend, I found my way to the little wooden church where Uncle Abe, for many years, had been so familiar as perpetual warden. Not wishing to intrude at so sad a moment, I waited at the door, while the little cortège wended its way up the hillside.

With bared head bowed low, Uncle Abe was following the humble coffin, but as he passed me, he stepped aside, and shook me so warmly by the hand that he left me wondering at his buoyant spirit in the face of such trouble.

The ceremony over, I ventured to call in at the now deserted cottage, only to find Uncle Abe home before me. The look of quiet joy in his eyes amazed me. Something in his throat, however, kept him from speaking, so when he motioned me to the chair which his partner had so long occupied, I waited for him to break the silence.

"The Lord's ever been good to me," he began at last. "Ben helped us through that bad winter you minds of, and now, she'll never want, whatever happens. I never prayed much 'bout particular things, Doctor, 'cept that. But I used to be askin' every day that she might be took first when the time come; I couldn't bear to think of her left to fend for herself, and now the good Lord's fixed it that way."

A little later, when I stepped out of that lonely cottage, I realized that I owed this man a debt which money could not purchase — the assurance that even we can contribute something is one of the durable treasures of life.

Ten more years had passed away. Uncle Abe had joined his devoted partner shortly after she left him, joyfully looking forward to that reunion with her without whom life was a blank to him. Our work had grown so much, and its cares and problems made such increasing demands on our time, that we had imperceptibly been losing touch with some of our fishermen friends, that personal touch which had been of such value to us. The vital channel through which one's life can best bless others had been almost choked with anxieties and "things." The advent of a wireless telegraph station had not been altogether an unmixed blessing, as it summoned one hither and thither, often on trivial quests. Even as our chains ran out through the hawse-pipes a messenger had rowed out to us with an imperious summons to hurry south, and settle some problems which the lateness of the season appeared to render immediately important.

This summer our boilers had blown out, and as we were unable to replace them for lack of the necessary funds, we had been obliged to cruise the coast in a small yawl. It had seemed an unmitigated catastrophe, for we had been delayed again and again by the fitfulness of seas and storms. But these very delays had given us time once again to visit round the houses, as in the old days. As we had flitted north, we had been detained at Capelin Cove for a couple of days, and had found the last of the old brigade, Uncle Ben, on his beam-ends. A severe stroke, twelve months previous, had incapacitated him for any sort of work, and now, as he put it, he lay "a helpless hulk," dependent on his poor old wife and only daughter to feed, clothe, and nurse him. As of old, he was too independent to ask aid from strangers, and his little stock had dwindled to the vanishing point. His wife, still "better to him than half a voyage," confessed that during the winter just passed they had been short of both fire and light. "Susie saws t' wood up when t' neighbors brings it out for us; but she isn't strong enough to go into the woods and haul any herself," her mother explained. "Ben has to be turned over a dozen times in the night, Doctor, and when it's below zero outside, and no fire or light, it do come a bit hard on an old woman, night after night. No, we haven't money any longer to reach to oil or coal."

Yet the whole atmosphere of the tiny cottage was infectiously cheerful. Uncle Ben lay beaming in his bed like a full moon at harvest. I was bidden to "sit right in," and share a cup of tea, the absence of sugar or tinned milk passing unnoticed in the genuine joy of the occasion.

Only as I rose to leave could I get a word in private with the women as to the ways and means for the future. "I suppose Uncle Ben's in debt at last?" I ventured, feeling certain he must have been obliged to abandon the old rigid law he had laid down for himself.

"No, no, Doctor. He'll never allow us to borrow a thing. You see he has no prospect of paying back."

"I see. If you could afford it you would buy some coal, oil, bedclothing, milk, flour, butter, a jacket, and — Oh, never mind making a list, now. I'm short of time, and I must say good-bye to Uncle Ben." Owing to his malady his speech was unintelligible; but there are other senses to come to one's aid, and the look in his eyes was full of peace and joy as he nodded "adieu." It sent me away grateful that a man with "nothing," had yet so much to give.

Mother Nature's arguments in Labrador are just as imperious as are those of Father Time with mortality, and three months later, once more, together with the fishing fleets of schooners, the birds, the beasts, and the fishes, we were migrating south at her bidding. It had been a troublesome summer. On some sections of the northern coast the fishery had been almost a blank, and we had left many friends anxious for the winter. A number of craft had been lost, in an unusually violent storm. The expenses of our own work had been heavy, and there were troubles in the outside world which seemed to render the raising of money for it particularly difficult. Telegraphic news from the home far away was disturbing, and we were being pressed to hasten on with all speed. We met nothing but head winds and high seas, and now the violence of the waves had forced us to turn back on our course and seek a temporary shelter. So we were glad enough once more to drop our anchors in Capelin Cove.

It was already late, indeed quite dark, before we had secured mooring ropes to the land, to enable us to ride out the storm in safety. Even now our little craft was rushing on the seas at the ropes, threatening, every time she came up short, to tear everything away with the jerk. Having done our best to make her safe, experience told us we had better get ashore while we could, in case worse came to the worst. It was much too dark to do anything more, and, worried and anxious as we were, patrolling the cliffs, with the rain beating its way up under our oilskins, only helped to add to the general sense of melancholy. So, telling the men to find quarters for themselves, but to keep watch, and call me if anything happened, I began to wonder how best to kill the hours which would hold no sleep for me. Suddenly my eye caught the glint of a tiny light on the hillside. It was Uncle Ben's cottage, and like a flash I realized that there lay the best source of comfort possible. Stumbling up the slippery rocks, I was soon tapping at the door of the familiar little cottage.

His good wife bade me a hearty welcome, though my dripping clothing and a howling blast of icy wind and rain greeted the opened door, tearing it from her feeble grasp. No sooner was it safely secured, however, than in her cheery way she led me to the old armchair by the bedside, for night and day were all alike to Uncle Ben.

I found the old man as usual, beaming all over with smiles. Suddenly a most unusual cloud spread over his features, as if he, of all men, was seized with anxiety about something. On returning to his bedside, I found him fumbling with his least useless hand in the bed clothing, and shortly he pushed over to me a bundle of dollar bills. Not realizing his meaning, I counted them and handed them back to him, telling him the amount. He at once signaled that this was wrong. So his wife was summoned to translate. It appeared that a few "things," like coal and sugar, had arrived for Uncle Ben while I was North; and he had at once suspected me.

His daughter, as teacher in the village school, was to receive forty dollars at the end of November. Uncle Ben had induced her to discount that sum, so that if I called in again and proved to be the guilty party, he at least need not be accessory to the crime of indiscriminate charity.

Uncle Ben's smile was radiant again, and he was trying to speak. "He says he don't want to go home owing anything," his wife explained. "He says you must have lots of others worse off than he this year."

I protested that it was merely a case of the windows of heaven being opened, and that the Lord had as much right to feed Benjamin free, as Elijah, or any other prophet.

Uncle Ben's physical eyes were dim, and I had taken care that the tiny oil lamp should throw no light on my features, but his soul was not to be deceived, and at the bidding of his eyes I submissively picked up the bills and ostentatiously put them in my pocket. The moments passed quickly as we talked of the old days, of the good times we had had together hunting, of Uncle Abe's discomfiture the day my retriever stole all his pile of ducks at Gunning Point and carried them to the hospital. Then we spoke of the future, till the old man grew as gay and blithesome, even in that sorry physical environment, as a boy of twenty.

There was a twinkle in Uncle Ben's eye when at last I moved to go that I could not quite understand. He seemed to be enjoying some joke all to himself. "He isn't satisfied about those bills, Doctor," his wife hastened to explain, as she saw my puzzled look. "He says that you have got to let him see you carry them away." Guiltily, I felt about for the bills, to satisfy him that I had no evil intentions, and was fortunate enough to find them under the chair cushion without his apparently detecting me.

I often picture myself now, like a whipped schoolboy, with my oilskins and sea boots turned into Etons and polished shoes, shamefacedly walking out of a master's study, parading the evidences of my guilt between my fingers.

On the verge of a long Labrador winter, from the threadbare cottage of a defenseless woman and a dying man, I was carrying all their material wealth. It seemed to stick to my fingers, and the synonym "filthy lucre," for the first time in Labrador seemed appropriate to it. For I was again realizing that I came away the debtor, and that this man who had "nothing" had still so many things to offer me.

Fortunately for my self-respect, there are more ways than one to Rome, and before we got our anchors for the home run, we had found a subterfuge which enabled us to circumvent even our friend's scruples, and yet make our message to him speak in those material terms which alone we felt qualified to use when dealing with Uncle Ben.

"You knows them cliffs, doctor, and you knows what them is."

7.
Rube Marvin's Confession
Down North on the Labrador, 1910

We had been enjoying a long three days' drive with our dogs through the finest part of the country, over the high white hills, crossing the frozen bays on the ice and sweeping down the courses of rivers at a pace that made it no easy matter to avoid the unfrozen rattles and rapids, as the dogs tore along the trail like a pack of hounds in full view of their quarry, with nothing in the way to stop them.

Night had overtaken us at the head of a beautiful bay where our lumber mill is situated, and the hard physical exercise of the journey had prepared us to enjoy to the full the generous hospitality of the manager's house, which was freely extended both to ourselves and our trusty dogs.

"Have they got the framing of the new schooner finished yet, Walter?" I enquired as we sat at breakfast.

"It's time they had," he answered, "seeing they had all the knees and timbers ready before Christmas, and the keel and dead-wood laid by New Year. I reckon there must be something wrong with Rube Marvin. He don't seem to mind if he does or doesn't this three weeks gone — and the boys can't get ahead without he's there to show them what to do."

"What can be wrong with Rube? I should think he had

less right to worry than any man in the bay. He ought to make quite a nice sum out of building the vessel. He isn't ill, is he?"

"He says he isn't anyhow, though his wife says he eats next to nothing, and scarcely sleeps any at nights. Jake Rumford says he thinks it's a touch o' the moon. They had worked a bit by moonlight to get all the knees out before the snow fell."

"What do you think of it yourself, Walter? It will be a bad business if we can't launch her before the men have to leave for the fishery."

"I can't say, doctor. He just seems like a man a mile away all the time, as if he was too far off to take notice of any one."

"Let's go and look at her anyhow, and perhaps I can help Rube some way."

So we donned our snow-shoes and crossed over to the sheltered cove on the shore of which the great white frame of the new schooner was silhouetted against the dark green background of the forest.

"Morning, Jake," I shouted to a man standing away up on one of the deck beams, "Where's Rube this morning?"

"Why, he was up here a second ago. Perhaps he's in the workshed there — though us generally works out here fine days."

Following his directions, I turned into the shed, and sure enough, there was Rube standing sheepishly by the bench, only too obviously having gone in to avoid us.

"Good morning, Rube. You're making a fine job of it."

"I'm glad you think so, doctor," he replied. "I suppose I'm doing my best."

There was such an utter absence of the usual twinkle about his eyes and the happy ring in his voice, and such a general tone of melancholy about him, that I couldn't suppress the retort — "I can't think you are doing anything of the kind to look at you, Rube. What's the matter? Not going to be hung, are you?"

Rube jumped as if he really feared such a thing, but as I could get nothing further out of him I went out and chatted with the rest of the men about the boat. I was at a loss to know how I could help him, for he did not seem anxious to speak of his trouble, though I knew well enough our foreman had something on his mind.

We had organized a big rabbit drive for Saturday afternoon, and a huge bonfire to be held in the woods in the evening, around which we were all to gather and partake of a feast in the open, prepared for all comers. Rube was crazy about hunting, and every one fully expected him to direct the shooters. But no Rube put in an appearance, and to me his noticeable absence cast quite a gloom over the proceedings. We had a fine tale of "bunnies" by evening, and as jokes were cracked and yarns told around the blazing log fire under the greenwood trees, hot cocoa and hot toasted pork cakes were passed around. Every one seemed just as jolly as sandhoppers. The frolic closed with singing, the voices of the men echoing through the silent forest. But for my part, my thoughts were all the time in Rube Marvin's cottage.

One of the men came up to me as we were leaving, "Can I have a few words with you, doctor, quite in private?"

"Certainly you can," I answered. "I'll get my racquets, and we'll be able to walk off the path. We'll be more alone then."

"Doctor," he began, "if you tells anything you knows is there anything in it for you?"

"What on earth do you mean?"

"I means, doctor, you's a magistrate, isn't you? And if a fellow tells of something done wrong, will them pay him anything for it?"

I had walked to windward, as the men say, while we were talking, and now I stopped suddenly and looked straight in the face of my companion. There I could see written in unmistakable language the expression of greed — so rare among our men, and so hateful, that I shuddered.

He was pawing the snow uneasily now with one foot, and his eyes fell before my gaze.

"Jacob," I said, "if you know of a crime and conceal it, you are guilty of it yourself in man's sight; and if you sell your guilty knowledge merely for private gain, you are doubly guilty in the sight of God — and of all good men, too. Yes, you can sell your soul and your honour, too, if you want to; there are plenty of buyers; but I won't let you do it without thinking of it again. Good-bye. I'm going back to the house." And I left him standing there motionless where he was, till I had turned the corner of the wood path, and he was no longer in sight.

Nothing further happened in the matter next day, and I tramped around the village from house to house as my business called me, wondering if I should hear more of the affair of the previous night.

The manager of the mill had built on to his house what he was pleased to call "the prophet's chamber," and in this I was wont to close the day alone, making up my note-books and finishing the day's round. The light shining through the windows apprised the people of the fact that I was in, and it was by no means unusual for some of them to avail themselves of the opportunity to come and speak about anything that might be troubling them.

I was glad that no one had come this evening, as I had so many things to occupy my mind, and I was just about to put out the light and "turn in," when a timid knock broke the silence, and in response to my invitation to come in, the door opened and the figure of my informant of the previous evening stood in the doorway.

"Shut the door, Jake, and sit down. I'm quite alone. No. No. Shake hands. You don't know how glad I am you've come out on top. Thank God for it, if ever you did in your life for anything."

He realized at once that I knew he had won out, for he looked me straight in the face and the beauty of a right purpose beamed out of his eyes so that to me it made the poor little room in which we sat better than a conqueror's palace.

"Doctor," he began, "it's about Rube Marvin. I knows

why he isn't hisself these days. He done a wrong thing two years ago, doctor, and he can't keep it to hisself no longer. I've been to see Rube since last night, and he wants to come and tell you all about it, only he can't bring hisself to do it."

"Then you have nothing to say yourself?"

"No, doctor, nothing, unless you or Rube wants me to."

"It's best that way. Let Rube alone, and let whatever he does come from himself and not from us. It will help him afterwards."

As I started out on my rounds next morning, I struck up the pathway from the side of the inlet — I had been obliged to walk on the sea ice owing to the thick trees along the land-wash — I heard the sound of children's voices, and found Rube's three little ones simply revelling in the crisp, dry snow and the bright sunshine streaming through the trees.

"Daddy dorn out," the oldest volunteered as she saw me heading for the front door.

"Where has he gone, dearie?"

"He's dorn in the trees ever so long."

I expected as much and went on into the house to chat with his wife as an explanation for my morning call.

As I tramped back along the edge of the woods and was nearing the Devil's Headland, I heard the crackling of bushes, and suddenly the tall figure of Rube strode out on his snow racquets into the trail ahead of me.

As I looked into his eyes, I could not help smiling at the transparency of these simple men. It was quite superfluous for him to begin without any other word of introduction — "I wants to tell you something, doctor. I wants you to send me to prison for it."

There was a long pause during which neither of us spoke. Rube was fighting for his life; I silent, lest I should rob him of the help which I knew would come to him if he won out alone. It was very cold, and the crisp crackle of the snow, as we strode along on our racquets, was for a full ten minutes the only accompaniment to the laboured breathing of my companion.

Suddenly he stepped ahead, and facing around, stopped me dead in the path.

"I done it!" he exclaimed almost fiercely. "I hadn't nothing for t' winter, and Downer promised if I did it, he'd give us all t' back debts, and a winter's diet for all o' we as well. He come three times afore I gived in. He were sailing for home t' next day, and threatened he'd take every bit o' grub away with him — and he would, too. He knowed what us had, and that us would be hungry before Christmas."

And the great strong man turned away from me, and burying his face in his hands stood there with his broad shoulders heaving, sobbing like a child.

"Rube," I broke in at last, "the best way is to play the man now, and regardless of what it costs, get this matter put right. Let's go to the mill, and you shall give me the whole story on oath. We'll have it properly witnessed, and then we'll send it off for good or ill to the chief of police in St. John's. If the worst comes to the worst, there are plenty of us who would see that Mary and the kids want for nothing while you're away." I put my arm in his, and we swung off at a pace I haven't tried to equal since. We seemed scarcely to touch the snow now, though only a minute ago it had clogged our footsteps like so much glue.

It was a strange party that gathered round the tea table that night. The two men to act as witnesses came straight in from their work, and I had dispatched a message to Rube's wife that I was keeping him for supper.

The following is the confession, taken and abridged from the long tale Rube told me:

"It was on Sunday evening, September 14, 19--. Captain Adam Downer came to my house after evening prayers and said he were going to sail from this place after midnight for the winter. He asked me if I had changed my mind, and would I help him to scuttle his schooner, the *Silver King*, and promised if I would do as he told me there would be no more said about it, as o' course he wouldn't and t' skipper didn't know nothing about it. He said it would only be t' skipper what would have to swear to the protest for t' insurance. He'd never know how 'twas done, and so he'd never be found out, and there'd be no need for me to get into trouble swearing lies.

" 'Come, Rube,' he says, 'don't be a coward. There's nothing to it. It's better than going hungry. You don't want t' kids to starve, do you?' Then he got up and took his hat and said, 'Well, I must be off and get some one else, if you's going to stand in your own light. I thought you had more spunk.' And then it came in my mind that it had to be done now, and some one'd surely do it, so them insurance folk would be no worse off if I done it than any one else, and why not Mary and my kids have t' grub as well as t' next man? And so I said, 'Well here goes.'

"We went on board, unknown to any one, and into the forecastle, where he had taken the ballast deck up. He lit a candle and showed me where to bore some holes in the planking, and I bored about a dozen, till there were only a shell left on the outside. Then us put back t' planking and roused all hands to get the anchor.

"It were a lovely fine night in harbour; there were no wind, and to get outside t' heads us had to tow the old *Silver King* in t' dory. Downer kept saying, 'There'll be lots o' wind outside, boys. Give her t' woodsails.'

"It were pitch dark and us couldn't see hardly what was happening, but us found a nasty cross lop running what made it terrible hard rowing; then jest as we was getting tired of it, something seemed all of a sudden to loom up under our lea, and us knowed we'd drifted with the southern tide in under the White Bear Cliffs. You knows them cliffs, doctor, and you knows what them is. Pull as us liked us couldn't even keep her head off shore. The skipper he was cursing Downer up and down deck for being such a ------- fool for coming out on a night like this, and swearing he'd lose him every cent of insurance if ever he lived to get alongside a magistrate.

"Meanwhile the roll of the sea on the rocks was making a

109

cruel noise and us could see the white of the breakers as they rose against the cliffs. Of course t' skipper never looks to leave t' deck, but even now the *Silver King* were beginning to roll heavy in the back-bound from the rocks. Us could hear him cursing Downer and telling he to get over in the boat and help save t' ship. But Downer were far too afeared to do anything, and at last t' skipper shouted to us he'd come in t' boat and do it himself, and give we a hand.

"Downer had no stomach for rough water, and he'd 'a' been drowned sure if the *Silver King* had struck. Yet I dunno, but I reckon Downer's prayers were answered somehow. For what we couldn't do for she, t' old schooner done all of a sudden for herself, and she come walking off again after we'd scraped along by the Devil's Headland as if she'd just been playing wi' we afore.

"There were a hatful o' wind now and t' schooner were slipping along well. Downer had said he'd take the watch forward, while t' skipper steered and us got a nap after t' night's work.

"It must have been just about coming daylight, though it seemed as if us had only just turned in, when some one touched me on the shoulder quiet-like, and I saw Downer leaning over me.

" 'It's all ready now, Rube,' he said; 'us is in near about to Roaring Meg wi' a fair wind in for Frenchman's Light. T' skipper's away aft at t' helm, and I've got the two half hundred weights way out along her bowsprit, and a line fast. I'm a-going to jerk 'em off so they'll hit her bow hard, and then I shall shout to the skipper for striking a piece of ice. You go at once and push out the rest o' them broken holes forward, and then I'll call to you to know if there's any harm done. You'll just shout out, 'She's stove in forward and sinking,' and then you'll run and tell the skipper. Only give her time to get down by the head a bit before he can come and see for hisself.'

"I was more than half minded then and there to up and swear at him for a devil that he was. 'Deed Downer saw plain enough I was nearly ready to go back on my word, and he just hissed into my ear, 'There's the holes that you bored in her now, Rube. If you goes back on me now I swear to God I'll have you in jail for trying to sink my ship. And I guess they'll listen to me, for I've got your bit what fits them holes stowed away feared I might want it.'

"If I'd had a gun, I believe I'd 'a' shot him then and there, for I seed I'd been fairly trapped. Then I began to think o' home and I sort o' half gave way. Well then Downer went on calling me a coward, and saying I was false to my word. 'Do you think they'll take your word or mine?' he said, till I just got up and knocked out the holes afore he was up the companion ladder.

"In a minute or two there were a huge crash agin her bow and I heard the skipper call out, 'What's that?' 'You've struck a pan o' ice,' shouted Downer, 'and I reckon you've stove in a plank. I'll rouse t' hands.' With that he jumped below, and seeing the water was already up to the flooring forrard and well above t' auger holes, he rushes up hisself and shouts, 'She's a-sinkin'. Get a boat out and let us save what we can.' The old skipper knew Downer for a coward and came forrard and peered over the fore-hatch hisself, and sees me with a hurricane lantern, peering round. 'Is it really bad with her, Rube?' 'Skipper,' I says, 't' boards is afloat already as you can see, and there's three feet o' water over t' leak. There's no man living able to save her unless t' pumps does.' 'Get up at 'em, ------- ye!' he replied. 'And Dick, too. I guess I'll stay and see if I can do anything below here myself.' And down he comes just as if he suspected something.

"Meanwhile, Dick mounted t' pump handle in less time than I cared about, and began pumping hard. I were afraid he might gain enough on t' water to give the ol' man below a chance to learn the real truth. But pump as hard as he liked, not a drop of water did he get. I soon guessed Downer had fixed the pumps — *in case of accidents!*

"As soon as Downer saw the skipper coming aft, he started shouting, 'For God's sake, help us to save the freight.

I'm a ruined man, if us can't save t' goods.'

"The skipper, he said nothing, but he put the helm hard up and headed in for t' bight. 'Skipper,' says Downer, 'seeing it'll all be lost, if you'll put her head up in the wind and let me save a few things, I'll give you half when we get on shore.' But the skipper didn't answer one way or t' other, but just held her right on for the headland. It did seem a *terrible* long time, but t' *Silver King* just wouldn't sink. A plucky ol' craft she'd been, and it seemed as if she just wasn't goin' to be killed. And I believe now she'd 'a' held on and got in to the beach and told her own tale if it hadn't been for that same ol' cross swell near t' land. For us could see t' skipper meant holding on to her till her sank, and no one dare even look up at t' boat without his leave.

"That were the worst time I ever saw — them hours doing nothing. Downer were praying. The dawn were breaking fast, and I could see his lips a-moving to hisself. For he daren't pray the kind o' prayer he were praying out loud for fear t' skipper'd hear un. And he were far too scairt anyhow, to move any farther than he had to from the boat. Anyhow, it got answered again somehow all right, for the very first roll that took the *Silver King* sent her lurching right over to starboard, and she never recovered herself one bit. Slowly and steadily she keeled over. There wasn't e'er a kick in her, and it were plain enough that it were her death struggle.

"Her big mainsail were under water, and there were no chance now even to get below to save anything. Lucky for him, t' skipper had sent Dick to get his kit bag for him in t' boat before and lucky for us all he saw Downer sneaking into t' boat. For I really believe he'd a cut t' painter and let her go fear she'll be dragged down with the schooner and he be damned forever and ever as he knew he ought to be. It's likely enough, too, he never would have got back to we, if he had once cut her adrift. But thank God he didn't, or I'd 'a' been in hell now too, having ne'er a chance for repentance."

At this point Rube suddenly stopped and there was a dead silence in the room — broken only by the scratch of my pen as I continued to take down his story. The thought of the awful peril he had run seemed to have robbed him temporarily of his power of speech. He sat for a minute or two with his head buried in his hands. Then apparently without even noticing the pause, he went on again.

"Well, t' skipper just wouldn't let t' boat leave the ol' *Silver King.* 'Stand by,' was his orders, and stand by us had to.

"There seemed no good any longer standing by t' ol' schooner. It was only foolish nonsense to be holding on if us were only just going to watch her go down. All of a sudden I guessed it. The port rail were going up and up and up, and t' starboard were already under water. Already we were almost climbing up her side, and I knowed if she didn't go down in a minute or two, the place where she'd been hit 'ud be out o' water. T' skipper knowed it too, I reckon, and all the time he were just enjoying seeing the fright Downer were in anyhow, and keeping it up as long as he could, while he were grinning to hisself that he'd find out yet what had done the damage to any craft in his care.

" 'Let go the boat, Rube,' the skipper called at last. I thought then even he were forced to leave her, for any moment she might dive down with all them rocks in her, and then she'd surely suck us all down with her. But no such t'ing.

" 'All hands in the boat,' he says. 'You and Rube take the oars and stand by till I calls you.' Now he was actually sitting on the side of the vessel, by the fore channel plates, holding on to the lanyards. The swell was a-lapping up over her and over him every now and again, but he seemed to take no notice that he was getting wet. Dick leant forrard and whispered to me, 'The ol' man's got a devil, I reckon, or he wouldn't be fooling any longer round this ol' bunch o' boards. And what's more the devil'll get him sure enough if he stays many minutes longer.' But all of a sudden again the truth of it came to my mind. The skipper had guessed it long ago: the ol' schooner couldn't sink for the air bottled up in her, and so long as it didn't come on to blow, she'd float about forever like a murdered corpse on the water. And what's more, her 'ud show every one where she'd been killed.

"It was dawn now, and bitter cold and shivery, when suddenly Downer called out, 'There's a schooner coming out of the bight. Seems to me she's a-coming right for us.' The skipper just looked round for a second. 'Maybe she is,' he said, and then he glued his eyes again on the schooner's forefoot which every now and then came nearly out of water on the swell. Not a catspaw of air now, only the swell of the sea.

"Once more the sweat nearly came out on me, for I thought that schooner 'ud surely be out to us and find out all about it. Downer were sitting in the stern. He looked the colour o' mud now, and he were praying hard to hisself again, and I know for what. It did me good to see him taking it so ill, for though I knowed I was as bad myself I just hated him, and hated him for driving me into it. And I knowed, too, even if us wasn't found out and was drowned, the devil would only be getting what was due to he.

"All this time the schooner were getting nearer. Us could plainly make her out now, heading right for us. At last Downer couldn't stand it no longer. 'For God's sake, skipper,' he kind o' prayed, 'let's be going.' There were no spunk left in him, and his voice sounded like a dog's whine.

"Old Abe were standing up high on t' schooner's side, and, looking round right into Downer's face — 'What's t' hurry?' he answered. 'She's been a good ship all her life long. She's served me well in many a tight corner, and I ain't a-goin' now to heave off and let her die alone. No, no, there's no hurry, *Mister* Downer. You and me 'll get safely back to land, don't you have no fear of *that*,' and he looked at Downer as if he meant a good bit more'n that.

"The light were only duckish yet, and it made old Abe loom up right large, standing straight up there on the schooner's bilge. It seemed almost as if he was t' preacher at t' meeting speaking, and us sitting there in t' pews a-listening. No one said nothing. 'Deed it was for all the world like a prayer-

114

meeting when the skipper hisself began to hum a line o' one o' the hymns us sings about — 'I hopes to meet my Pilot face to face, when I puts out to sea.' I thought Downer were going out of his mind now. He fair forgot hisself altogether like he done once at our revival, only this time he were shouting to t' skipper instead of to t' Lord. He started calling out, 'Why doesn't she sink? For God's sake, Abe, why doesn't she sink? Let's get away from her. I knows I shall die if I stays here any longer. I can't stand it. I can't stand it. You shall have all I owns if you'll only come.'

" 'Can't you think why she won't sink, Mister Downer?' Abe went on that slowly you'd think he were just beginning a sermon. 'Can't you guess why she won't sink?' Downer didn't answer, so the skipper did it for him. 'No, it ain't just cause the devil is in her,' he said, 'though I'm not saying there's not been enough devils in her to float her on a sea o' fire — on times,' he added. 'No, it's because she's got air in her bilge what can't get out. *That's* what's making her forefoot stick up that way out of water. I thought myself maybe it was just old Nick a-playin' with her at first, and I wouldn't wonder now if he was sorry to have such a trophy lost sight on — fear he might need to one o' these days just for a witness against people.'

"Downer's jaw dropped like at a wake when the cloth comes off t' corpse's head, and he pulled hisself together once more.

" 'We'll have to let it out, Abe. We'll have to let it out. She'll be a danger to the other schooners if us leaves her floating her.'

" 'Yes, maybe she will,' he said, but that slowly that I knowed well enough what he meant, that if any of 'em saw how easy it was to lose a schooner they'd likely do it themselves. Just then Downer suddenly looked up at the heads again, and there us could see a catspaw o' wind off the land and the sails of the strange schooner just bellying out and airing her aloft slowly straight towards us. Downer took it all in at a glance. She'd be alongside us in a few minutes if the breeze held on.

115

" 'Let's be through with it at once, Abe. It needn't take Rube two seconds to make a hole in the bilge. Here's the axe. And for God's sake, let's be quick, or I'll be dead o' cold, I knows I will.'

"But the skipper was not through with his sermon, and went on just as if he hadn't heard him.

" 'Yes, she'd be a danger to some on 'em, sure enough.

"I dunno whether Downer seed what he were driving at but to help him out the skipper added, 'Money be a shocking deceitful thing and there's no knowing what us poor creatures won't do to get it.' And then at last, seeing it was that cold and wet, he come slowly down and got into t' boat. For t' holes was now well out of water and t' white splinters was sticking out on t' outside.

"T' strange schooner were drawing nearer quite quickly now, and Downer couldn't stand it no longer. So grabbing the axe hisself, he ran forrard in the boat and climbed out on the ol' schooner's side, the devil o' fear sitting on his back. No one else said anything. Us just stayed as us was, while he started chopping at the planking, wild like. He didn't seem to mind what he hit so long as he got through, and he'd hardly begun before he hit an iron bolt and nearly spoilt his axe blade. My, he looked queer up there hacking and hacking like a wild man and as if his life depended on it. What's more, t' air in her made her something like a sounding box, and the noise must surely have reached the hilltops, much more the schooner coming towards us. Bang, bang, bang, went the axe. Meanwhile the skipper got into the boat and stood up in the stern with the steering oar in his hand, just waiting.

" 'Keep her close, boys,' he said; 'maybe she'll go down sudden when the fool get through her planking.'

"And so the ol' ship went down and us rowed in for the heads. The schooner passed us by without hardly noticing us, except one hand on the deck at the wheel waved his hand to we. Maybe they took us for a boat out fishing — maybe them didn't.

"That's all, doctor, 'cos soon as us got into harbour, Downer just told his story and nobody else said nothing. No, I dunno if he ever got his insurance. Most likely he did. The skipper could only have got hisself into trouble by saying anything, for he had nothing to show. He knowed nothing more than that he'd seen holes in her bow with the splinters on the outside, and the jury wouldn't care about that. It 'ud never have put Downer in jail, and so he let it go at that.

"No, I never got one cent or one cake o' bread. Downer cursed me for a fool as soon as I put foot on shore. He swore he'd never give me a cent, and if I said a word about it, it would be me what they'd send to jail for boring the holes. I couldn't have swallowed a bite of it anyhow, and it would have poisoned my family, I thought. So I just let it go at that. I had come to myself partly with the morning light, but I daren't go and tell any one, and it has been worse than being dead ever since."

There was a pause for a moment; and then I said:

"You've told me a lot of details, Rube. Do you remember it so well that you want to swear to it all?"

"I remembers every bit as if it was burnt into me," he answered.

"You understand I must send this on to St. John's, once you sign it, and that means you will be arrested and sent to prison, possibly next spring?"

"Yes, I understands it, and I'll be glad of it, too. I be a happy man once more."

I read over to him the strange tale he had told me, and then both he and Jake signed it, after taking an oath that the statement was the truth, the whole truth, and nothing but the truth. And there for the time the matter ended.

Rube went back to his work an absolutely new man. The crew of the new vessel didn't know what to make of it. Early and late he kept them at it, and she grew so fast that all doubts as to her being ready for spring were soon things of the past. The next time I went down to Rube's little cottage, his good wife told me he almost beat the baby sleeping now, and if it weren't that she hauled him out of bed in the morning to go to work she reckoned he'd sleep the clock round.

But meantime the big envelope with the "story" in it was winging its way around our barren coast from dog train to dog train, and ever getting nearer dread courts. Knowing as I did their desire in St. John's to temper justice with mercy, I had ventured to attach an appendix of my own, humbly praying that the voluntary confession, the man's otherwise clean record and sterling character, the dire results to his innocent family if he were departed before the fishing season, might all be taken into account and the warrant for his arrest delayed until the fall at least.

The arrival of the first mail steamer is always a matter of importance. One may almost say the whole settlement runs riot with excitement. But it certainly was if possible heightened this spring to me when from among my letters there fell out a long, solemn-looking, blue envelope, stamped with the royal crest and official insignia of the Supreme Court of Justice. With almost trembling fingers I tore it open, and then to my joy I found that my petition was granted, and Rube was not to be sent up with the witnesses for the trial of Mr. Downer on the charge of barratry, till the following October. This would give him a chance to get the season's fishing for his family.

The case came on in due time. Downer was sent to prison for two years, Rube for one. But when I was passing through the next spring on my way north, just as the fishing began once more, a petition we presented to His Excellency the Governor for the King's pardon for Rube was successful. I had the infinite joy of carrying the news to him in the penitentiary myself. I found him in excellent spirits and perfect health, and as I shipped him as a hand on my steamer the moment he stepped out of prison, and as I walked down the street with him myself to the boat, he felt the coming out into the world again less than, alas, many a poor fellow does. He has been one of my best friends and helpers from that day to this, and to-day I know of no man living on our long coast whom I love more, whether he be in broadcloth or fustian, than my ever happy and optimistic colleague, Reuben Marvin.

Sir Wilfred and Lady Grenfell, 1929. "I knew neither whence she came nor wither she was going, nor why she was in black."

8.
In Double Harness
Forty Years for Labrador, 1932

In June, 1909, I had finished another long lecture tour in England trying to raise funds, while my colleagues had the hospitals and dog-driving on the Coast. The time had come to sail westward again, and I was dreading the ordeal and saying goodbye to my aged mother, perhaps for the last time. I had begged her not to come again to Liverpool to see me off, that I might avoid the long, slow parting as the ship left the dock, and the loved form got ever smaller and less distinct till it disappeared.

New ideas are rare, but suddenly a brilliant one flashed across my mind, in answer to my despondency. Why not take my mother with me to America? True, she was seventy-eight years of age, had been born in India, and had lived a very active and exacting life. I was to receive an M.A. from Harvard, and an LL.D. from Williams College. It would make the occasions ten times as enjoyable to myself to have her share them. She would be far more thrilled than if she received degrees herself — and if — well, she could sleep just as peacefully on one side of the Atlantic as on the other; while I knew that the generous Americans would love to see her and welcome one of the real saints of earth.

My earliest and most devoted volunteer worker was Miss Emma White, of Boston. Today, twenty-five years later, I can recall seeing her, straight from her desk in the office of the Congregationalist Library, entering St. Anthony, sitting on the bow of a schooner which we had built in our mill, while written below was the legend of her own name, in whose honor the ship was dedicated. Miss White is still at her seat in the Library, but her soul is still in Labrador.

Her advice was sought and taken on the question of my mother's visit; with the result that we sailed together on the *Mauretania* for New York. The Cunard Company gave my mother a lovely suite of rooms, with a great four-poster brass bed, which, little though I knew it at the time, was to serve me well in the most monumental adventure of my whole life.

The *Mauretania* took four and a half days to reach New York. On the second day out, a delightful Scotchman, with a burr as characteristic as a bagpipe, introduced himself to me with his family. He had been born in Stirling, and his name was Stir-r-ling, and he lived in Chicago. He valued life, exactly as I did, for its glorious opportunities, and he played shuffle-board (deck tennis not being invented), took afternoon tea, and when we talked said worthwhile things, having travelled much and been 'educated' and not merely informed. One girl was a graduate of Bryn Mawr University under the famous Miss M. Carey Thomas as President, the best-known women's university in America. Her sister was as charming as herself, and we hobnobbed naturally, for both were full of gaiety and humour.

My own activities in life had engrossed my whole being so completely that the idea of marriage had never entered my head. Now I am uncertain as to whether we should or should not take a course in the philosophy of it. My own experience says very decidedly 'No'; but after twenty-odd years of married life I am not sure either whether this decision should be made public by the husband or the wife. Anyhow, marriage came to me 'out of the blue' — the true blue itself — and a new, happier, and more useful life began. A surgeon considers it justifiable to record end results long before over twenty years have elapsed. Why not a layman? Anyhow, the above is the most sober opinion of a mere husband and of one who knows that no celibate has any right to speak on this subject.

These intervening years have been characterized in civilization by an almost miraculous advance in human knowledge — also in divorces, failures to enforce laws or commandments, and in the apotheosis of self-expression. The relationship of one to the other of these or their causes I must leave to my readers, asking them to remember that, from my viewpoint, human knowledge, except that based on experience, can never be a correct criterion of wisdom.

I am aware that there is no special virtue in keeping the Ninth Commandment, not to envy your neighbours their happiness or their goods, when one is fully occupied otherwise. As for special providences, personally I never pray for a fair wind for my hospital steamer which might mean a head wind for the schooners. Beyond asking for God's good hand upon my unworthy self in everything, the marriage problem in particular had never been a petition of mine for any special providence. I still think, however, that it came more graciously as it did.

By the third day out, a fact that previously had never caused me any worry got on my mind. I was on the 'greyhound of the Atlantic,' and those interested in the pool on the day's run had been completely fooled, for the *Mauretania* had set a new day's record of over six hundred miles. The universal hustle of our American cousins had often amused me. Yet here I was, becoming acutely conscious that I stood in sore need of it myself. 'Ships that pass in the night,' with courses presumably as different as the girl's and mine, might never meet again; while the captain assured me in triumph at dinner that we should land in two more days!

As for 'the girl in black,' I knew neither whence she came nor wither she was going, nor why she was in black. Indeed, all

I did know was that she was down on the passenger list, and also with the dining-saloon steward, as 'Mr. Stirling and family.' An old school friend on board at that time, manager of Lord Northcliffe's great pulp interests on our Coast (Sir Mayson Beeton), jokingly quizzed me when I was late for an appointment one night, as to how I came to be walking round with 'the girl in black,' the handsomest girl on the ship, and what her name was. I wondered why he asked me. But as a matter of fact both of these were questions, which, according to Hoyle, are considered taboo at certain times. So we let the name go as 'the girl in black.'

As to her name, had I had any doubt, although I am not considered to be lacking in courage usually, I am certain that at that particular time I should not have dared to ask Mrs. Stirling. Necessity has no respect even for a coward heart, and I realized that twenty-six knots an hour demanded action. To take the more venturesome of two paths has always been an axiom with me, and I remembered what that splendid old patriot, Nehemiah, put on record. When the Persian tyrant noticed that his mind was low, and asked him if he wanted anything, he knew that to make a petition displeasing to the King involved immediate death. He records, 'I prayed to God, and I said to the King, may it please . . . ,' all in the same breath. Well, I did the same thing, and in return received the real shock of my life. 'But you do not even know my name!' The name of a Labrador reef does not matter. You have only to avoid it, anyhow, and it probably has a dozen, for conferring names is a favourite pastime of explorers. But now on that account I seemed to be in real danger of shipwreck. Even a perversion of truth could not help me, convenient as that may be in time of trouble, for I knew I could not stand catechizing. Labrador seafaring habits, however, came to my rescue, for they had accustomed me, on the spurr of the moment, to act first and think after. 'That is not the issue,' I answered. 'The only thing that interests me is what it is going to be.'

Years later, 'the girl in black' told me that once at Bryn

Mawr she was invited to come and hear a medical missionary talk about Labrador, and that she had refused in no unmeasured terms. I thought at the time there at least was possibly another reason for my faith in providence in small things.

I have known even Britons who are not at their best on the rolling wave, but such genius as our family has displayed has, so history assures us, shone best on a quarterdeck, and on this occasion it pleased God to add another naval victory to our annals. Perhaps no previous suitor had tried to carry her by assault. Perhaps Nelson's greatest victory was when he put his telescope to his blind eye, ignored all suggestions to the contrary, and just went for the enemy, as at Copenhagen. That has been the family way, anyhow.

The generosity of my friends, considering the mental abnormality that characterizes this not uncommon experience of life, will condone in me a wicked satisfaction that my lack of appreciation of the blessing of a rapid voyage was paralleled by the joy that my mother preferred that blessed brass four-post bed to even a chair on the promenade deck. When, just before landing, I told her that I had asked a fellow passenger to become my wife, I am certain, had the opportunity offered at the moment, she would have tumbled down the *Mauretania's* grand staircase again as she had once done when bidding me goodbye at the pier in Liverpool. But that invaluable four-poster proved a stabilizer, and, though her equanimity was plainly upset, it only showed itself in an unaccustomed tear rolling down her cheek — one of the tears I cost her that at least brings me no regrets.

When the girl's way and mine parted in that last word in material mêlées, the customshouse shed in Manhattan after the arrival of a big liner, I realized that in reality an armistice only rather than a permanent settlement had been achieved. True, there was no stern father in the case, but there was a mother and a home, both in Chicago and at Lake Forest. These loomed up as formidable strongholds for a homeless wanderer

125

to assault, especially as I had no alternative to keeping a whole series of appointments essential to my work among the fishermen and just postponing the 'campaign on the western front' until later. Moreover, the fact that there was neither brother nor sister, niece or nephew, to fill the void, if I carried off 'the girl in black' to the other end of the continent, was a very serious consideration. But the inexorable schedule that kept me in the East, and the generous hospitality of friends that meant so much to my mother, afforded the blessing that work always carries with it — an occupied mind, though the greatest of all ventures loomed up as more and more momentous as the fateful day drew near for me to turn my face westwards.

This visit to my wife's beautiful country home among the trees on the bluff of Lake Michigan in Lake Forest was one long dream. My mother and I were now made acquainted with the family and friends of my fiancée. Her father, Colonel MacClanahan, a man of six feet five inches in height, had been Judge Advocate General on the staff of Braxton Bragg, and had fought under General Robert E. Lee. He was a Southerner of Scotch extraction, having been born at Nashville and brought up there in Tennessee. A lawyer by training, after the war, when everything that belonged to him was destroyed in the Reconstruction Period, and being still a very young man, he had gone North to Chicago and begun life again at his profession and eventually become head of the bar. There he had met and married, in 1884, Miss Rosamond Hill, daughter of Judge Frederick Torrence Hill, of Burlington, Vermont, but who, since childhood and the death of her parents, had lived with her married sister, Mrs. Charles Durand, of Chicago. The MacClanahans had two children — the boy, Kinloch, dying at an early age from tuberculosis of the hip joint. Colonel MacClanahan himself died a few months later, leaving a widow and one child, Ann Elizabeth Caldwell MacClanahan. She and her mother lived the greater part of the time with her sister, but she, alas, had also passed away a year before.

The friends with whom my fiancée had been travelling

were next-door neighbours in Lake Forest. They made my short stay doubly happy by countless kindnesses; and all through the years, Mr. Stirling gave me not only a friendship which meant more to me than I can express, but he also came to Labrador to study our problems and gave his loving and invaluable aid and counsel in our work, as well as endless help, until he too crossed the divide in 1918.

At Lake Forest, in spite of my many years of sailor life, I found that I was expected to acquit myself in many activities I had left long ago to landlubbers, among other things, to ride a horse, my fiancée being devoted to that means of progression. The days when I had ridden to hounds in England as a boy in Cheshire stood me in some little stead, for, like swimming, tennis, and other pastimes calling for coördination, riding is never quite forgotten. But remembering Mr. Winkle's experiences, it was not without some misgivings that I found a shellback like myself galloping behind my lady's charger.

My last essay at horseback riding had been just eleven years previously in Iceland. Having to wait a few days at Reikyavik, I had hired a whole bevy of ponies with a guide to take myself and the young skipper of our vessel for a three days' ride to see the geysers. He had never been on the back of any animal before, but was not surprised or daunted at falling off frequently, though an interlude of being dragged along with one foot in the stirrup over lava beds made no little impression upon him. Fodder of all kinds is very scarce in the volcanic tufa of which all that land consists, and any moment that one stopped was always devoted by our ponies to grubbing for blades of grass in the holes. On our return to the ship, the crew could not help noticing that the skipper for many days ceased to patronize the lockers or any other seat, and soon they were rejoicing that for some reason he was unable to sit down at all. He explained it by saying that his ponies ate so much lava that it stuck out under their skins; and I myself recall feeling inclined to agree with him.

The experiences of those days in Lake Forest live in that

part of one's mind that surely does not have to be replaced every seven years. Something somewhere in the human make-up does not get destroyed this side of the grave, whether memory is a window through which spirit communicates with body, or whether it is a library, proof against every kind of oxidizing process, slow like that always going on, or fast like that by fire, I do not know.

Achievement or failure, not doles or accidents, have always loomed up in my experience as the dominant events in my life. I thank God for this terrestrial achievement. A ring had sealed the fact of success. But 'the girl in black' has just looked over my shoulder and says, 'No, I can't let you put that down to your land accomplishments. Let's call it another Grenfell naval engagement.'

Our wedding had been scheduled for November, and for the first time I had found a Labrador summer long. In the late fall I left for Chicago on a mission that had no flavour of the North Pole about it. We were married in Grace Episcopal Church, Chicago, on November 18, 1909. Our wedding was followed by a visit to the Hot Springs of Virginia; and then, heighho, and a flight for the North. We sailed from St. John's, Newfoundland, in January. I had assured my wife, who is an excellent sailor, that she would scarcely notice the motion of the ship on the coastal trip of three hundred miles. Instead of five days, it took nine; and we steamed straight out of the Narrows at St. John's into a head gale and a blizzard of snow. The driving spray froze onto everything, till the ship was appropriately sugared like a vast Christmas cake — another providence. It made the home which we had built at St. Anthony appear perfectly delightful. My wife had had her furniture sent North during the summer, so that now the 'Lares and Penates' with which she had been familiar from childhood seemed to extend a mute but hearty welcome to us from their new setting.

We have three children, all born at St. Anthony. Our elder son, Wilfred Thomason, was born in the fall of 1910; Kinloch

Pascoe in the fall of 1912, two years almost to a day behind his brother; and lastly a daughter, Rosamond Loveday, who followed her brothers in 1917. In the case of the two latter children the honours of the name were divided between both sides of the family, Kinloch and Rosamond being old family names on my wife's side, while, on the other hand, there have been Pascoe and Loveday Grenfells from time immemorial. Only an insane man could expect one personality to possess all the talents valuable for perfect work. Nor can two possess them. Our experience, however, is rather Einsteinian than Newtonian. Twice one has been more than two in personality. Looking back on twenty-three years, marriage has been a geometric rather than an arithmetic factory in my records.

'The girl in black' was a born organizer. Her Scotch ancestry and her college career together certified that. Organization needs, besides patience and expenditure of energy, a peculiar vision, not specially granted to the seafaring mind. Order has a new quartering on our shield.

In old days my best friends often felt like holding back help because they feared the work could not 'carry on' without the founder. There is little doubt of that now. Each department — and how many new ones there are! — runs by itself. 'What every woman knows' is literally true in every normal Scotch married life. More than once, I've heard 'the girl in black' called 'Maggie.' Nothing in these days of depression has helped us more than the orderliness of the ramifications of this work and its many scattered little offices, and the fact that so many important posts are held by volunteers. I used to feel that all my responsibility to the public for their help was ended if we did the work to the best of our power and as economically as we could. I had to learn that was far from enough, and 'the girl in black' has shielded me by her highly trained business capacities from many troubles. An autobiography is a book of confessions. Our work would not have been where it is today, without 'the girl in black.'

By bringing into coöperation the personal service of so many of her highly trained friends, the Child Welfare Department and the Educational Fund, the management of which has been one of her special interests, came into being. It was good to educate the children who had no others to guide or provide for them. It was an imperfect service not to equip them with the mechanical training that would fit them to avail themselves of the opportunities of their country and enable us to expand our work.

Every autumn 'the girl in black,' besides her own family, mothered a batch of boys and girls from Labrador to institutions from Truro Agricultural College, Nova Scotia, to Berea in Kentucky, including Pratt Institute, New York, Wentworth Institute, Boston, Rochester Athenaeum, Upper Canada College, Toronto, and to business and technical schools wherever she could personally secure the necessary opportunity. Everything from an outfit, a route, a ticket, and a personal guide had to be arranged. I have a photograph of her on a truck with sixteen students who had just reached Sydney, in Cape Breton, 'for distribution.'

Her determination to keep open house on the Coast, and how through the years she has been able to add that to her contributions, I must leave to 'wops' and workers and visitors and people. I counted fifty-eight at the *al-fresco* supper after the usual Sunday evening 'Sing' on one occasion, and twenty fishermen to a sit-down dinner in the sun porch at another, and I thanked God.

In the keeping in touch with friends and helpers, in her courage and vision in discovering new ways of earning instead of begging help for different activities in turn has lain, however, her most unique contribution; for even in a thankless task like raising money to keep our work going, she prefers any honest labour to the dole, and has shown that many love to give work who could not possibly give money. I venture to suggest that not a few of the most successful of her efforts have been new features in the missionary world.

Everyone uses a calendar. Millions are sold. Why should not a Mission make a better one than anyone else? The conception and the venture on twenty thousand, so as to cut the production cost to a minimum, were due to 'the girl in black.' The artist of King George's Christmas card did the original painting. Raphael Tuck, internationally famous for art reproduction, did the technical work. But the vision, the venture, the hardest work of marketing and the amazing result of eight thousand dollars to the funds were due entirely to 'the girl in black.' Thirty-five hundred unsold copies remained. The covers were removed, framed, and sold as souvenirs both on the Coast and at home. The fifty-two photographs of Labrador were divided between souvenir picture albums and covers for charming boxes of candies, and the publicity and profit from these are still being returned to Labrador.

A congestion of industrial goods made some new method of marketing them imperative. We knew they were what the public wanted, and that they were worth the cost. A new idea came to the rescue. Why not secure a truck, get volunteers to drive it, and arrange summer sales at holiday resorts in the foyers of hotels? It all sounds so easy now. But there were a thousand difficulties at first, and the amount of writing and personal interviewing, and the preliminary outlay, which was large, all needed hard work, business acumen, and vision, and a peculiar courage of naturalness. Perfectly splendid girl volunteers rallied round, sales were organized from Florida to Maine. New power was given to the workers in Labrador to give out more labour and to many more children and poor women the gospel of the love of God was preached in actual loaves and fishes. But the *fons et origo* was once more 'the girl in black.'

Again hers was the launching of Dog-Team Tavern, twenty miles south of Burlington, on a Vermont highway, to be furnished free, to be run by volunteers, who cleared its unavoidable overhead expenses by selling teas to tourists and washing up dirty crockery for the love of God, in order to help market products of industrial work made by far-off fishermen. This venture shows the same faith exactly that brought the same results, and in the same ways, that Paul speaks of in the Epistle to the Hebrews, and that many a Christian never believes could be accomplished outside the Bible. Such things are not looked for today. Yet this whole effort also has materialized exactly as it was dreamed in the heart and mind of 'the girl in black,' who has mothered it like many another from the first. Those who have so nobly served in it longest are the first to realize this, that the fact that many visitors have come all the way from New York, Boston, Philadelphia, and from farther to visit it, suggests its success, and raises hopes of a similar work in winter in cities, and perhaps on other highways, and in the service of other good causes as well as ours, in the days to come. The Dog-Team Tavern is advertised by pointers over one hundred miles of road. Volunteers produced them and put them up. Think of Jonathan Edwards considering a volunteer Scotch girl, and another from Texas, and another from Bryn Mawr, driving an old borrowed car around New England and nailing up pictures of dog-teams on posts, as being 'preachers of the Gospel.' Anyway, we do.

Our telephone this afternoon announced: 'Your head worker is in the hospital here. Her car skidded and turned over twice.' Lady Grenfell telephoned three hours later: 'L----- is back at the Dog-Team Tavern again. She crawled out of the window after the car made two somersaults, got forty men to turn the car right side up, and she has limped back to the Tavern in it, with only a cut and a bruise or two.'

Even as this book goes to press, there are two new ventures on the tapis to help us carry on in these days, difficult for all the world, but especially so for a population like ours, small, isolated, and even before the depression, living often close to the hunger line. This time it is puzzles, made specially for us by Raphael Tuck, of London, and 'containing two hundred pieces of the polar regions, to help build up the work in Labrador,' and a bazaar, undertaken at the suggestion of

Miss Phillips, of the Animal Rescue League. With her help and that of other generous friends, this fair is to be held in Boston in November. Both these efforts call for courage and for untold work, but knowing 'the girl in black,' I have faith to believe that she and her colleagues will put them through. What do I think of marriage? What do I think of my digestion? I consider it a pathological symptom to think of either. The title of this chapter best describes my experience. I once watched a large camel and a tiny cow harnessed together in Egypt, and doing excellent work with a plough. I feel like the smaller partner, grateful for redoubled capacity. In every way marriage is as natural as any other condition of life on earth. Like Labrador, the 'early explorers' said, 'It is of no use to man.' We think, however, that it was they who were no use.

No thinker can believe for a moment that the worthwhileness of life is what we get out of it. No one who enters life, or school, or club, or country, or marriage, possessed of that spirit, will find any human institution a success. Mere physical beauty certainly does not ensure permanency of love. It cannot. It does not last. Yet marriage has made it last. Look at Darby and Joan — hand in hand at the eventide of life, facing together the last experience of us all with the same smile with which they faced the first. Is that a failure? An inevitable cause of failure of all human ideals is selfishness. Call it sin if you wish: I am no stickler for labels. Whatever you style it, 'self first' is the negation of the *raison d'être* of our being on earth at all. It and lasting happiness, married or unmarried, are as incompatible as alkalis and acids, or perhaps better, as fire and gunpowder.

Like business, sport, ventures of all and every kind, marriage to be a success must be entered with a will to succeed, as must faith in man and even in God. The incidents of a day must be looked at in due perspective, not as to their little reaction of myself, whether it is *my* ease, *my* stomach, or *my* dignity, but the effect on the other half — the team. Only one selfish player in the best team on earth can lose the game if he

133

'hogs the ball' when he should pass it to give another player the glory of the touchdown. We two, anyhow, are signing this chapter together. When we began, we believed marriage to be a part of God's plan for men's and women's happiness on earth, enabling them to help the world just so much more, since union means more strength and wisdom and courage. Now that we are on the last lap and the final goal seems not so far away, we are holding hands closer than ever, confident that the final experience of life also will be easier to face thus, and indeed become only another joyous venture, when these worn-out bodily machines of ours shall be discarded, and on the other side we shall work again, in new fields, together.

Lady Grenfell.

Grenfell admires a monument to Rameses II in Egpyt. "It sounded like a fish story, but he had discovered unopened tombs at the very foot of the pyramids."

9.
Global Travel
Labrador Looks at the Orient, 1928

All quests are better for an objective. Ours, therefore, should be to try to see everywhere we journeyed the results of the efforts of other human beings to meet the challenge of life. How fascinating to be able to view entirely from outside, the things that other folk take pleasure in, the ends for which they live and strive, the ways they express themselves in customs, habits, and productions, the attitudes of the minds of men who live in sunny zones to those same old impulses which give us our peculiar characteristics in the frozen North, the expression of their faith and hope, the ways they seek for courage, comfort, and consecration, the forces from without and within that are making for righteousness and a better world.

* * * * *

To visit Thebes, oldest and greatest of cities of Egypt, is still like a day in London for interest. It has a history of five thousand years, and many splendid words have been written about it. With its temples, the finest in the world, it is a place for the dreamer of dreams. Here dwelt the god Amen Ra, the Jupiter of Egypt. There Alexander came to be pronounced son of Amen, so as to make things easier with the people whom he had conquered. It proved a really diplomatic move.

Mut has a temple here. Oddly enough she is the goddess of truth, which is recognized by a feather in her hat. There is no mention of Jeff. Thebes dwindled away when the capital moved nearer the mouth of the Nile, and eventually went to Alexandria. The Temple of Luxor is another monument to the whims of men of long ago. With our new methods of building, we run up skyscrapers while they would be putting up one pillar. Records left in the buildings do but little to make us realize the awful cost in human life of these places, while their pictures, showing great kings, so called, clubbing miserable fellow beings to death in honour of blood-lustful gods, make one half sorry they have not anyhow all been forgotten long ago. The desire to revel even in pictures of these horrors seems morbid and reactionary, and except for the research student the real interest is purely historical.

Far the most interesting to us, however, was the story of King Ahknaton, who revolted against the degrading materialism of the priests and their villainously harmful conventions. Apparently, the teachings of his mother, a foreigner, inspired him to this. He strove to have his people worship not Amen Ra the sun, but Aton Ra, the power that gives life to earth and shines in love upon all the world through the sun. He was a pacifist, and the gory pastimes of his predecessors sickened him as much as they do us. He managed to move his court from Thebes and build up a new capital at Tel el Amarna. That is where we found most pleasure, dreaming over what might have been the fate of Egypt if only the Egyptians had followed this great man, the 'heretic king,' or 'the lunatic king,' as many call him. His city and court were built on the usual magnificent scale, much as Akbar built the city of Fatipur Sikri, which like Tel el Amarna was deserted on his death. For though the young king, weakening in health, held out bravely to the end, the priestcraft, as it is well named, ultimately triumphed, and not only on his untimely death were the priests able to move his young son and everything pertaining to the court back to Thebes, but soon were able also to get rid of him altogether and assume the regal power themselves. This son was the famous Tut-ankh-amen.

* * * * *

One of the huge colossi erected by Rameses II in modest memory of himself is said to be vocal. The legend is that every morning it makes a sighing sound complaining to its Mother Dawn of the brutalities inflicted by Cambyses the Persian. At Esnâ an old temple is being slowly dug out in the middle of the town. Only the portico, however, is as yet visible, for a natural land boom followed the discovery, and the people whose present houses are built on land that overlies the roof refuse to sell except at such prices as antiquarians cannot pay. Endless huge bats clung inside the roof of this old building, and the noise they made was like that of a large chicken house. Close by is the temple of Ed-fû, the most perfect in Egypt. It is one hundred and fifty yards long and the propylon wall is one hundred and fifteen high. We climbed onto the roof and got a perfect view of the town and country around it. There is a fine marsh here for hunting geese. Good hunting can be had in many places in Egypt, not so much on account of the protection of game through the ages as owing to the destruction of the people who hunt.

On the wall of the temple at Komombos are the carvings of some surgical instruments, scales, spatulas, lancets, forceps — quite an outlay for nearly two hundred years before Christ. Here also were some dried-up crocodiles, sacred in this part of the country at that time. In fact, animal life was apparently regarded by many as more sacred than human life; dogs, rams, cows, birds, lions, wolves, jackals, beetles were all worshipped.

* * * * *

The bazaars of Cairo are fascinating. They are a great collection of shops carrying every conceivable variety of handicraft work of every queer Eastern design and material. Gold jewelry shops are so especially numerous, one would at first suppose that the people were almost indecently wealthy, especially as one sees so many veiled women, and always unaccompanied, haggling over purchases. The fact is a husband has only to say to his wife, 'You are divorced,' and the marriage is annulled. He need show no reason unless her relatives are powerful enough to make him. The law, in order to protect these poor women a little, allows them to take with them their present jewelry. The Government guarantees the value of the gold, so into that go all a wife's little savings. Of course, money so hoarded is idle and produces nothing for those who so sorely need every piastre, but the custom is old and seems still to act as a soporific on their needed courage to fight for better justice.

The beaten brass and copper work, the beautiful gold, silver, and copper inlaid work, the wood and ivory inlay are marvels of meticulous craftsmanship. We saw tiny boys of seven and eight years producing exquisite results, while we saw many barefooted craftsmen working on similar articles with their fingers and toes, especially weavers. . .

Of course, the greatest antiquarian attractions of Cairo are the pyramids and the monolithic column at Helipolis . . . We loved them best when we saw them under the auspices of Dr. Reisner, of Harvard, from his camp at Gizireh near by. He had been fourteen years at work, and to us was the inspiration which the optimist always is . . .

Only a few weeks later, and once more we were guests at the Doctor's camp. It sounded like a fish story, but he had discovered unopened tombs at the very foot of the pyramids, and Cheop's steward and secretary, if not the great Cheops himself, after some six thousand years in his grave, had been safely landed once more on the bank of the Nile. The Sakkarah pyramids were also intensely interesting, as were the tombs of the prophets at the site of Old Memphis far out in the desert, tombs built in the Sixth Dynasty, away back before history begins, and thirty centuries before the great Rameses of Moses' day, whose colossal statue we also visited, saw the daylight. The Sphinx was recently restored and further discoveries made about it. The rock was imperfect and Cheops would not use it for his pyramid, so he abandoned it. His son Chefhuen saw its possibilities and worked it up into a Sphinx, with a red body, a white hood, and a natural-colored face and eyes. The people worshipped at an altar between its front paws. Thothmes IV was asleep between the paws once, and dreamed that it complained of the weight of sand that was upon it, so he had it restored. The head has been unsafe, as sand and weather had nearly cut off the neck. Now it has been repaired, except the face, which it seemed impious or inartistic to meddle with.

It was interesting to learn that the building of the great pyramids had exhausted the resources of Egypt as much as the longest wars. They occupied a hundred thousand men for a lifetime. The Cheops Pyramid is said to weigh five million tons, all hauled to the spot by the contractions of human muscle cells.

* * * * *

The extraordinary building known as the Church of the Holy Sepulchre [in Jerusalem], with its quarrelling shareholders, may one day cease to be a scandal in the name of Christianity . . . We felt how small our own sacrifices in life for Christ have been, compared with those of these countless thousands, who through the ages have made pilgrimages to this spot, to say nothing of rich men like Godfrey and Baldwin, heoric knights, who left everything, and chose to be buried here at the foot of Calvary.

Somehow, though, it is so entirely different from anything that has actuated our own lives that, if we must tell the truth, we went away with a feeling that, if Christ came to the Church of the Holy Sepulchre today, He would, as of old, sweep out all these shams, swindles, and palpable falsehoods, as making His house into a den of thieves rather than a house of prayer. To give offense hurts everyone, and these words will, I fear, offend some readers. I must ask them to remember that we realize our own shortcomings, while we respect every man's real faith, if it is one that is evidenced by its fruit. There would be no use in this record of our attempt to learn more about the coming of the Kingdom of Righteousness if we did not chronicle truly our own reactions to these 'religious centres.'

* * * * *

We decided to spend Christmas Eve in Bethlehem. It is a clean, prosperous, and picturesque little city, also set on top of a rolling hill. We were guests at a fine Church of England school for girls, who happened to be home for their holidays. The site of the inn where Christ was born is at the very end of the road overlooking the valley, and has been the seat of a khan or inn for unknown centuries. It is one of the very few sites of almost unquestioned authenticity, and it must at least be near the old Caravanserai of which we are told in the Gospels. We watched a great procession, composed mostly of Latin Christians, come out from Jerusalem. The Greeks observe a later date for the Festival of the Nativity. Bethlehem was *en fête*, and the day warm and sunny. The boys swarming up the railings and lamp-posts to get good views, the children in gala dress batting toy balloons, and the women from various districts with their curious gay headdresses, made a brave and interesting show. All kinds of people made up the procession, thin and fat, lay and clerical, of all ages and sects. Many countries were represented. We spent our afternoon in the Shepherds' Fields, climbing down the stony and precipitous path, the very one along which the wondering shepherds went 'up even unto Bethlehem.' There was no question among our ladies when we reclimbed it in the evening that the shepherds' phraseology had been correct. One of our party, as we climbed, noticed a shepherd driving his sheep into a large kind of cave with an open mouth. In reply to her question, he said: 'I am putting them away for the night to be safe from the jackals and dogs.' But she objected: 'There is no door to the cave.' He replied simply: 'I am the door.' It is the Eastern shepherd's custom to lie down across the doorway of such caves, and with his own life to protect the sheep. The incident took us back in thought nearer to the Master than all the glory of tinsel decoration of shrines erected to Him, or all the attempted exactness of locating the places where once He had been, but which now showed us little evidence of the presence of the Prince of Peace.

* * * * *

Like everyone else who is interested in India, we considered our interview with Mr. Gandhi while we were in Delhi a great privilege. He is a man who for good or evil has been a large factor in the life of his country during these past six or seven years. We felt there is no reason to question that his motives are sincere, unselfish, and absolutely well intentioned. He is certainly an example of self-government that many of his critics would do well to copy. You cannot be in his presence without feeling a real affection for the spirit of the man; he seems so human in the very best sense of the word. That is one reason why so many hearts in India have been touched and drawn toward him. India's masses need and yearn for something deeper than they find in the average rational, utilitarian official. Other reasons are that every one likes to feel grown-up, and many think that, however bad a government may be, so long as no alien is a member of it, it spells freedom, while many more are merely eager to have a share in it themselves. Our interview taught us why India cared when Gandhi lay fasting for their sake. They loved the man who, being literally rich, showed his love by being willing to become poor for their sakes.

* * * * *

It is hardly necessary to say what we think of India, its fruits, its flowers, its unequalled gorgeous blooming trees, its exquisite villages which, especially in the South with their thatched roofs and quaint architecture, just melt away into the palm groves and mango orchards. Who that has lived in London and New York and possibly haunted, as I have, Threadneedle Street, Bishopgate, or for years the purlieus of Whitechapel around the London Hospital, who that has suffered from the overpowering masses of humanity which seem to walk on one's head in Wall Street or crowd one into nothingness in the Bowery, can do aught but love the streets of India with their gaily clad crowds which scintillate with colour like the Aurora Borealis of our Artic sky in the fall of the year? Look at the butterflies which flash past one in the sunlight. Where can you find their equal anywhere in the world except perhaps in Madagascar or in South America? The colouring of the birds of India is almost unparalleled. The vivid greens of the paroquets add beauty and lustre even to the gardens of the Taj Mahal or the palaces of Delhi and Agra and Fatehpur Sikri. The dazzling blues of the jays, the iridescent reds of the kingfisher which one sees on every river bank, to say nothing of the glories of the national peacock, the impeyan pheasants, the friendliness of the Mina birds, and the sauciness of the crows, and indeed of all the animals in the country where animal life is held absolutely sacred, all leave a never-to-be-forgotten impression on one's mind.

He who for most of his life has had to take his morning dip in the polar current, often between pans of ice, does not fail to appreciate a bath in the luscious breakers of the Coromandel beach. He who has lived among fishermen, whose potential captives are limited to codfish, herring, and a few salmon, cannot but value a visit to the aquarium at Madras, where there are fishes which excite alternately every emotion of which humanity is capable, from their almost unbelievable variety of shape, colour, and habits. We can never forget a cruise in a small rowboat in the Bay of Bengal watching the ridiculous antics of solemn regiments of exquisitedly delicate white mullet rising in clouds from a blue wave and flitting through the air like a miniature march-past of soldiers, to be followed by some huge skate jumping out of the sea high into the air and crashing back, with the noise as of a cannon exploding, in his attempt to rid himself of parasites.

* * * * *

'See Fijiyama and die' is almost the first epigram of Japan. We drove to it from Tokyo by way of Lake Hakone and over the Miyanoshita. This route gives you the great advantage of seeing this overpowering and unique mountain with the foreground of the lake in front, while the more modest mountains in the middle distance only seem to enhance the majesty of this hoary-headed monarch. If you can catch him with the sun setting behind him, spare no effort to do so. It is often difficult to catch him at all, as impenetrable clouds seem bent on shielding his glories from the profane eyes of the world below. The water in his top, nearly half a mile wide and over twelve thousand feet in the air, occasionally causes a burst of steam, suggesting the awful powers latent in his mighty head. Little wonder so many pilgrims go there to worship. We drove all the way back from Miyanoshita a third time to see him and enjoy once more the mountain road twisting in hairpin turns through endless forests, on past the many rushing cascades and waterfalls that seem so fitting a setting for the foreground of this monarch of mountains.

Grenfell amuses two children patients with a stethoscope.
"The body's story is by far the most wonderful in the world."

10.
The Healthy Body
Yourself and Your Body, 1924

Nothing on earth is so valuable to a man as a sound body. The old Romans held that in a sound body dwelt a sound mind. We can go further and admit that the actions of a soul itself are influenced by the health of the body, for it is only the soul's machine, and it is the soul's only machine on this planet. More sins are the result of defects in our physical machine than we can realize.

The jelly, or protoplasm, out of which it is made becomes granular or fibrous when it should be clear or elastic, and then, like a steel axle that has gone granular, we tell it, as usual, to do one thing and it does another. Very ordinary habits, like the pleasure of a good meal, grow on us till they become a physical sin, just as the habit of drinking whiskey is acquired very easily. Alexander of Macedon, the conqueror of the world, lost his life by overindulgence in eating fish called lampreys. This kind of suicide is just as bad as any other kind, and is a sin against life itself.

Having two sons who had just reached the age of ten million Whys? and Hows? and Whens? and Wheres? it occurred to me that they would respect the development of their bodies more if they understood more about them; and that they certainly should be as much interested in the perfection of their bodies as in that of their studies of birds or collections of postage-stamps. Man naturally prizes what it knows to be of personal value to himself, and will not willingly allow it to come to harm. We still know little enough about how to perfect our bodies. But the recent discoveries of the enzymes, endocrines, the vitamines, the hormones, and many other agencies which influence bodily development, or at least protect it from a thousand dangers as do sera, vaccines, antigens, and so forth, make us increasingly realize how much more we can do to add a cubit to our stature and years to our time on earth than once we dreamed of.

As we begin to know what infinitely marvellous conglomerations our bodies are — combining every kind of machine on earth into one, and then outclassing every one of them — we also begin to know how easily they can be irretrievably spoiled. Moreover, when we find that the most wonderful regulations of the body and its functions are so essentially material that even its subtlest govering factors, like adrenalin, can be made out of ordinary coal tar, or, like thyrodin, out of seaweed, we realize more our responsibility and opportunity for its rational care.

The wise Greek adage, γνῶθι σέαυτον (know thyself), can and should be made now to include at least a bowing acquaintance with so individual a personal possession as our bodies. How many people discover all too late that their bodies have been irremediably injured through their own ignorance. Alas, innocence does not save from the inevitable retribution of physical sin. If the greatest Christian saint puts his finger in the flame of the candle it will be burned exactly like that of an every-day sinner. If you *will* put very hot things in your mouth and swallow them to save the pain of burning your tongue, you will get an ulcer in your stomach whether you are an aged multimillionaire or an impetuous "sans culotte."

The body's story is by far the most wonderful in the world. Marvellous things are built by men, but this is more wonderful than a fairy palace, for every brick is alive, and the parts make themselves. It is the only real automatic machinery in the world. Moreover, the units make their own rules; choose some to govern the rest, while they train others to do all the repairing, feeding, draining, tending the pumps, and manufacturing of everything needed from a drain-pipe to a seeing-machine. They do all their own cleaning. They keep their own police and maintain armies to protect the whole machine. There is nothing they do not do.

Yet much has been left to us. Have you ever thought that if we had enough strings in our ears so that they could hear every sound that fills the air, we should soon be stone-deaf? No instrument on earth could stand it. So it is left to us to invent the telephone, and gramophone, and radiophone, in order to catch and give us just the sounds we want; or the microphone or magaphone, to enable us to use louder sounds or hear those only when we want to which are so low that we could not otherwise know of them. Again, if the eye could see everything there is to be seen, how very soon we should all be blind. So to us is left to make ourselves microscopes and telescopes and fluoroscopes (X-rayscopes), so that we can pick out exactly what we want to see, and only when we want to see it, and also so that we can see through apparent solids.

We who dwell in these bodies are also intrusted with the even higher honor, that of helping to build a better world. Now if you take a bit of iron, or hydrogen, or even gold, all you can make out of it is iron or hydrogen or gold. However, if you have two different things, you can, in time, make many things — just as hydrogen and oxygen combined make a new substance altogether, called water — or carbon and hydrogen make paraffin — or yellow and blue make green. So carbon, hydrogen, and oxygen make starch, or sugar, or vinegar, or a thousand other things. Take a cell and divide it equally and it will become two cells exactly like the first; but take a cell and add something to it, and it may become your body or mine.

Here is a story. A friend of mine, a dried-up, tough old

Indian general, slipped off the platform at a station one day, and the train ran over him. It cut off both his arms and both his legs. People rushed him off to the nearest hospital. Some hours later he swore before a magistrate that he was still he.

"He could swear that he was still he."

Every one, even the wise old judges, agreed that he was he, though he had lost the larger part of his house — or his machine with which he used to 'connect up' with what we call 'this world.' Of course his walking-machine parts were gone and his holding-on parts were gone. But he still had his talking parts, so he could swear all right that he was still he.

Remember that our bodies are not we ourselves. Contrariwise! They are ours. We lose bits of them sometimes. We often spoil parts of them, and some people spoil the whole of them. That is terrible, isn't it, when we should be making them the very best bodies we can. They are the most useful possessions we will ever have, and they are all our own. The building of our bodies is largely in our own hands. We are the general managers and responsible for them and for everything in them.

Of all the pictures I know, one somehow helps me more than any other. There was once a poor doctor, but a very earnest, fine man. He noticed that the lives of people who *milked cows* with a kind of rash on them, were spared, when that terrible scourge called 'smallpox' was killing one in ten of the population of the world. He loved his little baby boy as much as your father does. But he was so splendid a knight that after he had taken every possible precaution he decided to put some of the poisonous composition into the body of his own little boy to find out if it really would save children's lives. The picture is of him trying that — and it did all that he hoped. Doctor Jenner will never be forgotten, because directly and indirectly he has probably saved more human lives than any other man who ever lived.

So begin by knowing all you can about, and holding absolutely sacred, your body; the only one in which you can face that great adventure that men call life.

Grenfell finds a quiet moment to sketch the magnificent Labrador scenery. "What in our heart of hearts could be the true answer, fear though we might to confess it and dread though we might to face it?"

11.
What Christ Means to Me
What Christ Means to Me, 1927

In the autumn of 1891, a friend suggested my visiting the fisheries on the Newfoundland Banks, so in 1892 I sailed in the 99-ton ketch *Albert* to the Newfoundland and Labrador coasts. The conceit of the suggestion, the expense of it, and the question of qualifications for the undertaking worried me not a little. As a mere physical adventure the opportunity seemed almost too good to be true. I consulted my beloved mother as to what she would do. Her answer assures me that now, though so-called "dead" she still speaketh. "I would use daily," she replied, "the words of the 143rd Psalm, 'Teach me to do today the thing that pleases Thee'." Could any theology be more profound? Any sociology more practical? To do my surgery as Christ would do it! My navigation, my investigations, my study of the new problems which would confront me! I am sure that when Christ made doors and windows in Nazareth they did not jam and misfit.

I have been discouraged sometimes in the Labrador work by men who would say, "Why spend money for X-rays, radium, and up-to-date hospitals for a few fishermen?" Yet these same men never queried, "Why hang the price of a full-fledged hospital in pearls around my wife's neck as earlier barbarians did?" Why? Because that is one of the first things that Christ means to me. He does not do work cheaply because He is dealing with simple men whose bread depends on physical health, nor let things slide because human experts are not there to criticize. Would any decent man? There is no question as to what Christ would do. Wouldn't He work to secure the right clay if He needed any for the cure of a working man's eyes? I've spent many dollars on pilgrimages to famous clinics, and many on instruments and new books with the idea that Christ would at least have me a modernist in the practice of surgery.

What a homecoming that was in December, 1892! What a splendid trans-Atlantic trip we had made, when the ice of approaching winter drove us out of the Labrador harbours, offering us six or eight months in Jack Frost's bonds, without supplies, as the only alternative. We averaged seven and a bit knots per hour from harbour mouth to pier head in England, all the while dreaming dreams of answering as soon as spring came the most alluring challenge I had ever pictured in all my visions of opportunity. Hero? Bunkum!! That pedestal will not stand the test of experience. One thing the people had to have was nurses — skilful, trained, gentle nurses, the best exponents of love when it is most needed and most vital. The first two of my old nurses who were asked to volunteer responded at once. Good positions assuring an income and a future, were already theirs. But the love of God, like contentment, never fails to turn the wooden cup to gold and the homely whistle to a strain of sweet music. The splendid description of love in even the first Epistle to the Corinthians, Chapter xiii, fails to envisage its infinite power.

Two years ago, our little hospital steamer, after twenty-five years' service on our somewhat inclement coast, sank incontinently at sea almost without warning. I found just such a one as I wanted — small, seaworthy, well-found, rating 100 A.I at Lloyd's, and with boilers which would keep steam so economically on wood that I can run her a mile on a twelve foot stick, once we have gotten steam up. Her owner was compelled to sell her. She was within our means, and I bought her lying on the hard at Southampton. No steamer so small, so far as I could learn, has ever crossed the North Atlantic. She is only sixteen feet in the beam, having about thirty inches of freeboard, and a coal bunker capacity of only eighteen tons — about an hour's burning for a modern trans-Atlantic liner! "You haven't money enough to pay anyone to take her across," commented more than one wiseacre friend, after the news of her purchase leaked out. But I was not worrying. I was appealing to a higher force. Skilled friends as soon as the chance was offered them brought her out "for nothing, just to do their share." If that skipper volunteer and that engineer volunteer did not share my creed, ought I to have refused their help, which was *real* help? Could that offer, made in His Spirit, to do as He would do, be irreligious? And would a decision to refuse their help because "I knew it all," and as a result have the boat stranded in the other side and our people left without its aid, be religious orthodoxy? It certainly would not be Christian. Every day we cruised in her last season on the Labrador Coast, I thanked God for that spirit of His which works in this world "without observation" and without labels, "That moveth where it listeth."

This is not an effort to tell a story, but to try to analyse one as better evidence than any mere statement of what Christ has meant to one human being. Already enough has been said of self. Ninety-nine hundredths of the Labrador work has not been mine at all. To say that it is a movement in which I have been allowed to share is more accurate. At times I have wished I had more money. As the years went by, the sense of the resulting slowness and waste of time impressed me increasingly. I realised how slowly new ideas come to one's mind. Often I have wished that one could have taken a course at some University on "How to love your neighbour." Surgery, because it was one's own particular line of work, a remedial effort which, after all, only left patchwork, was almost necessarily over-emphasised. The need for pro-phylactic work, child welfare work, industrial, educational, mechanical engineering, cash stores, means for thrift, the value of artistic influences, the stress on efficient propaganda, the dignity of collecting money, have in turn all gotten up and shouted to me. Christ has become to me to mean more and more, *doing* something, anything, well.

The medical mission really has nothing over the engineer. Clewes of India was as efficient as Gilmour of Mongolia, or Paton of the Hebrides, or as Livingstone in Africa. Tyndale Biscoe with his hunting-crop in Kashmir has built character as surely as ever did Stewart in Lovedale, Higginbottom and his famous agricultural farms in India, Jackson and his reindeer herds in Alaska, as much as Hudson Taylor and his men in China, or General Booth and his drums the world around. There is no such thing as size to weep over. Size after all depends as Einstein shows on velocity; and so we can see how the spiritual is real, the real is spiritual, and the widow's mite bigger than all the gold and silver of the Pharisees. Mrs. Wiggs at home on the cabbage patch is as true a hero as Sir Lancelot with his spear on his quest for forlorn damsels. God's challenge to us is only to do whatever we can. Christ's religion is as natural as the flowers in spring, and relates to the everyday things around us.

I can remember being blamed because my critics claimed that starting a lumber mill in order to give labour to hungry families, was not a rightful use for "mission" funds. Not a few criticized us severely for so problematical a venture as introducing reindeer into Labrador. When we accepted a gift of a site for a hospital on Caribou Island, Labrador, the deed stipulated that I must not sell pork or molasses, or enter into trade there. At that time it seemed an insult to an English surgeon that he had to sign his name that he would not go into the grocery business. But the time came when it was apparent that that was exactly what Christ would do in that situation. Most of the necessities of life had to be imported in Labrador.

The people lived on a truck or peonage system, and were paid in kind and not cash. They did not know the value of the fish they caught or the price of the things which they were buying. I remember being bitterly assailed for sending the *Trade Review* telling the prices of our produce and our necessities, into different sections of the Coast. I was openly pilloried because I collected a series of "accounts" spread over a period of years, and analysed them in order to assure myself of the ability of the country to support its people. Indeed, I once became so discouraged with the poverty and recurring diseases of both children and adults, diseases which resulted from malnutrition and chronic under-feeding and lack of proper clothing, that I journeyed to British Columbia and made an agreement with the Prime Minister to send over two hundred families to sites selected on that seaboard, he to advance the passage money and see that they got a fair start. This, however, the Newfoundland Government of the day refused to permit. When at length we actually preached cooperation, and started a cash co-operative store, we at once became anathema; and when later we started such a venture four miles from a trader's station, he, an ex-politician, set wheels in motion not only in the press, but in political circles, and a commission was sent down purporting to inquire into our activities, but really with a view to disclosing our economic turpitude.

Personally, I never felt that the Sermon on the Mount, or the healing of the blind and lepers, brought Christ to the Cross. It followed so closely after His actual interference with the money changers, that I have no doubt but that the devil of greed for gain which still ruins so many of our men in power, had most to do with His enemies coming out into the open. That devil is not dead yet, not by a long way!

We have now many new efforts seriously commenced, and are trying to tackle our problems more in the light of modern sociological teaching. We admit our crudity, and we fully endorse *its* wisdom and indeed, most generous volunteer experts are enabling us to give somewhat efficiently those interpretations of Christ in action. A lesson much needed and one which true love calls for, is always to be optimistic. Never again will I be pessimistic because I cannot see the Christ bringing in His Kingdom in my way. If my boy promises me that he will not smoke, and I find a used pipe in his coat pocket, I do not say anything, I just trust him.

Now, whenever we have a real challenge to a real problem, we have learnt to believe that the harder it looks, and the less material return there seems in it, the more surely and easily we find someone to respond to its challenge. The fact is, humanity naturally responds to SOS calls when it hears them. There is something else in man besides original sin. Experience has demonstrated this unanswerably.

The storm tosses even the best of ships and sometimes just hurls her on the rocks, or, striking some snag, she becomes partially disabled, and if unaided, is driven ashore in spite of her best efforts though she may have been once classed "100 A-one" at Lloyds. During the years, more than one human craft, damaged in the treacherous currents of modern social life, has come North to seek help in our less artificial surroundings and they have found it, and gone back, and are living new lives today. But each time, so it has seemed to us, it has not been the escape from the temptation, but the obvious challenge to get up and help others, the chivalry of the Christ service, calling even to heavily handicapped and almost lost talents to do worthwhile deeds. Deep calls to deep. Never yet have I seen the fear of punishment help a prodigal to a new sonship.

There may be sections of the world where the method of presenting the Gospel of Christ to men which prevailed a couple of centuries ago when actual information was necessary, will function to some extent today. But in the new light of our modern world it seems too cheap a price at which to purchase so great an end. If Christianity cannot be attractively presented to the world, if its preachers are not leaders in deeds as well as in words, if our presentation of Christianity has nothing beyond its philosophy to offer to life and fails to "deliver the goods" which developing reason and enriched faith in God teach mankind, then mankind has a right to demand some new religion which can adapt itself to our ever advancing world. I can never believe but that in every man is born a spirit that is a real, as well as a potential sonship of God, though defects in the human mechanism through which it has to relate itself may pervert its efforts and prevent its demonstrating itself. These defects may be hereditary or "original," and are often a visiting of the sins of the fathers on the children in the most terrible of all possible ways. As I see the Christ, He teaches that the task of making life worth living is not a loafer's job. The slacker is not only miserable hereafter, but harmful and foolish here and now.

Life is like Labrador, a Labourer's Land. It is intended to produce that which no loafer's land ever anywhere can ever produce, the character of sons of God. Can anyone desire a world better suited for that task? Christ teaches us that life offers a worthwhile prize to us all, but like all other valuable prizes, it has to be won always with some temporary self-sacrifice. Love, Joy, and Hope and Peace are the slow growing fruits of the spirit. Love spells sacrifice. True joy spells achievement. Hope thrives best in hard times. Peace is a result of victory first over self. The most meticulous emphasis on the letter of Law or Gospel is more likely to kill than to make alive. The way of the Spirit, exactly as of the flesh, in a world like ours, spells labour — hard labour, whatever the end we seek.

The western world which listened to, and heard, if ever so indistinctly, Christ's message, has led in its emphasis on the dignity of labour, for Europe is still somewhat handicapped by certain social customs and human relationships which are relics of barbaric days. The newer world, in partially freeing itself from many of the old incubuses, was trying to give expression to what Christ really meant — brotherhood under God as contrasted with the snobbery and pride of hereditary rank and its dangerous anachronisms. That mere possession of things still bulks so large in the new world's psychology, is her

159

greatest danger today. Perhaps Christ's truest message was the emphasis He put on labour. He was a labourer and most of His disciples were also. To be repositories for the truth for which He came to die, He chose mostly not the rich, but the labouring men. I have personally found more inspiration in the cottages of fishermen than in many palaces of the rich. Many of my most helpful and richest hours have been in the company of these children small in the world's eye. Paul felt the same. He saw the value of labouring as a tent-maker.

Christ means to me that this world has the potential in it of a Kingdom of God. We are finding this through working men, not mere talkers, men too humble as a rule to set themselves up as oracles. I take off my hat to every man of science always, if he is a man who works: Newtons, Clarke Maxwells, Stevensons, Darwins, Huxleys, Faradays, Humphreys, the Wrights and Bells, Marconis, and Edisons, who by work teach us of the marvels of the world; and so help us to realise that it is the work of God. What we know of this world with our finite brains this side "the Divide," convinces me that neither man nor chance created it. My faith at any rate does not have to strain itself to the breaking point to accept that premise as a sound, working hypothesis. I take my hat off naturally also to men of physical accomplishment, the Spartans, the Olympic victors, the great athletes of all time, for their ability to do things. To revere that prowess is more natural than to revere a dollar, a dinner, a diamond, or a drink.

It is mostly in the West that this reverence for physical accomplishment has flourished. Alexander and his Greeks failed to convey it to the Indians, or the East generally. It may be a side-light, but it seems to me a direct reflection of what Christ's messages really mean. "I am come that ye might have life and might have it more abundantly." He never meant to me the Christ pictured in the art of the middle ages — the convent, the monastery, the hermit, the recluse, the body hampered here with religious clothing and furniture, or hereafter with harps and halos. He means that we are the sons and heirs of the

Maker of this marvellous cosmos and are the channels upon it of His Kingdom to be. I want to believe this anyhow, and the wish itself seems some presumptive evidence that there exists in me something beyond the "mere material," that is if the "material" does exist. The objective is big enough and the conceit lofty enough to suggest an answer to what is the meaning of life, and to redeem it from being the hopeless self-determined tragedy which some are willing to accept, and to lie down under.

The very idea that we can make life worthwhile suggests an answer as to the meaning of life. For through the third great department of life, the world with all its doubts, with all its scepticism, so often only the retribution for its failures, is increasingly trying to keep those passions under, the conquest of which is half man's glory. It proclaims increasingly as real victors, the men who have triumphed in the spiritual strife, and won out against the sloth that damns and the assaults that kill. The fame and honour of a Lincoln, even as against a Washington, grow from day to day. The spirit, portrayed in the "Perfect Tribute," of the speech at Gettysburg wins instant admiration from ever increasing hosts of mankind.

So as we think of men who were great — great with the greatness that explains the real challenge and opportunities of life, there rise to our minds, not Midas and Croesus, creators of money bags, not Caesars and Alexanders and Napoleons, creators of temporary kingdoms, but the men who have had a part in however a restricted walk in life, in contributing to the great Kingdom of God on earth, the men and women who embodied most nearly the spirit of Jesus Christ. That spirit made over the Johns and Peters, and Pauls, the Cromwells, and Lincolns, and Jeromes, the St. Francises, the Savanarolas, the Luthers, the Cranmers, the Kingsleys, the Wesleys, the Livingstones, the Careys, and the Martyns, and later the Booths, the Taylors, and Gandhis, the Sadhu Sundar Singhs and all those who have followed the Christ. Following Christ is a hard task. It is a warfare. But He teaches me increasingly that

161

life is worthwhile if and only as we make its goal "well done" and not "well comprehended."

It never worried me whether I believed infallible Pope, infallible fundamentalist, or infallible teacher of science that is current. Christ ever meant to me a peerless Leader, whose challenge was not to save ourselves, but to lose ourselves, not to understand Him but to have courage to follow Him. The religion of Christ is the simplest and most human course of life, as well as the most divine. Life is not the horrible tragedy of being bound to a wheel from which escape into a Nirvana of forgetfulness was the loftiest hope. Life is a victory to be won by the will even against a timid intellect. Life is always everywhere a real, tough, courageous fight, with daily opportunities to which are added all the fun of achievement and all the glories of the conqueror. The edges of my own intellectual conceit often got jarred. But the lure of the real meaning of life and the absolute confidence that my faith was not mere credulity was a constant help. Common sense is divine sense after all — our youthful attitude to religious conventions was not so far wrong after all. I realise it was because we had wrongly thought of religion as banished from practical affairs that we had dreaded nothing more than being considered "Young Christians" by our fellows. To imagine that Christ would not wear flannels and play football, or a dress suit and attend dinners and functions, or accept the innocent changing conventions of the day, is as irrational to me as to suppose that we ought all to wear Quaker dress or a Sadhu's petticoats, or that Eskimo women should affect long skirts. In fact, it goes further than that. The Christ I visualised is inconspicuous for all absolutely unnecessary differences. He would wear no jewellery of fabulous value any more around His neck than in His nose. No ostentatious show of any kind was His. He hated titles, separating man from man. Leadership in everything that was of value for body, soul, and spirit was His. He was the last on earth to be anything snobbish. He was the Captain of the team, the Solon of scholars, the most modest and unobtrusive in social life. He loved play and work as well as worship. I could not love a Christ as divine, Who did not. So for me the interpretation of Christ has had to aim at all that. The conventional pictures of Christ were and are abhorrent to me. All ideas of hair shirts and unnecessary ascetic habits in connection with Him are repulsive since they are unnatural. An incompetent "other worldly" Christ has no attraction whatever for me. Viewpoints that many better men than I still affect, for me are impossible and radically incompatible. Thank God I realised in time that some men see red as green, and others green as red. Some men live for grand opera. I only go to sleep in it. Some men love things because they are rusty and musty and old, and see nothing beautiful in a thing simply because it is useful. I have seen some patients to whom a drug means life and had to be devoured daily, while to another the same drug in the same dose spelt death. Some traits in our characters are, I firmly believe, due to hereditary faults in our interpreting machine. There is truth in the deductions of the Chicago jurist that much wrong-doing is the result of physical deficiencies. The head of a great college in India, whom I know, cannot tell the difference between red and green. Yet he is a most valuable worker. This knowledge has saved me many an ill-timed, unkind, and entirely wrongful judgment of others. It is the answer to "Why so many denominations?" and "Why any bitterness between them?"

Even before I entered the work among fishermen, I decided that for my part, I would never ask a man whether he believed exactly as I did before I could agree to work whole-heartedly with him. If we wait until our thinking machines are all in complete accordance before we co-operate, we shall never work together in that universal brotherhood which must precede the coming of the kingdom of God on earth. The emphasis on intellectual interpretation divides us — the willingness to work together draws men together. And it is wonderful how hard it is, looking at the manner in which men of diverse faiths have met their problems, and interpreted divine love in their deeds of every day, to judge as to the way in which they say their prayers or get their inspiration and strength, or what particular labels they should bear in the religious world.

Illustrations by the score leap to mind as this thought comes to me. To refuse the help of a surgeon, a nurse, a teacher, or an engineer, in a position where no interpretation of love is more needed than that which they can render, and as an alternative to allow one's fellow creatures to suffer for lack of what they offer just because I believed differently than they would be to my mind not only criminal but the very reverse of what Christ did. When did He, Who sent out Thomas and Judas to preach the Gospel, ever impose any such test? He might have done so. For He had a wisdom that no man has ever been able to question. But He did not, so why should I? Surely the call to go out and help the Lord against the mighty is the call most likely to find response in human hearts. Only the dead feel no answering emotion when helplessness appeals to them for what they can give. Who would not want to rush for the child about to be run over in traffic, or to save the victims from a burning building, even if it were only a suffering cow or chickens? There is something that responds as naturally as an automatic reflex to high ideals and can only be called love, though it is undeniable that one can in time so destroy and impede the physical channels of impulse and response, that some degenerates even seem to be incapable of anything divine. We know that faulty machines do cause us to both act and speak wrongly, and that damage done by chronic indulgence not only makes restraint necessary in the case of chronic criminals, and drug addicts, and lunatics, but also causes mechanical defects to be transmitted to children; which is the same as saying that these exceptions need help and power from outside themselves. Christ's unparalleled confidence in Judas, it always seemed to me, was what broke at last the traitor's heart, even if too late, but broke it all the same.

Christ to me is the justification and inspiration to keep my body and mind fit and perfect that thereby I may preserve myself, my soul, fit to accomplish, able to serve, and confident I shall hear over there, not "you are loosed from the wheel of life, you can now enjoy forgetfulness" but "well done, here are more talents for you, and more victories to win. Enter into that kind of joy which is the joy of your Lord."

Christ means to me a living personality today who moves about in this world, and who gives us strength and power as we endure by seeing Him Who is invisible only to our fallible and finite human eyes; just as any other good comrade helps one to be brave and do the right thing. Faith was essential for that conviction fifty years ago. Today with telephones and radios and X-ray, and our knowledge of matter as only energy, there is not the slightest difficulty in seeing how reasonable that faith is. "The body of His Glorification" passed through closed doors, so the Apostles said — well, why should I be able to see it any more than I can see an ultra-violet or an ultra-red ray or molecule, an atom, an electron or a proton? All that those old fellows claimed was that "now we see through a glass darkly, but then face to face."

Christ called for faith in Himself. He never called for intellectual comprehension. He sent out to preach His gospel men who had not any creed or any intellectual faith, only a dumb sort of faith that Christ was more than man. I believe that He sends me out also to help make a better world. Surely that is not an irrational conceit or sentimental twaddle. Christ says that we must begin with faith, but that we can prove the truth of that faith ourselves.

It is not extraordinary that we must begin with faith. It is natural because we have to begin everything else with faith. Faith is an inherent quality of finiteness. It cannot be foregone. We cannot live without it. We cannot make any progress without it. No faith, no business; no faith, no fun; no faith, no victory. But we can make Christ's faith knowledge in the same way that we can make it in any other realm, that is by testing it in the laboratory. All new treatments of men's bodily ills I have

165

been testing in that way all my life. I get treatments from anyone and everywhere and try them out. That is all that my Christ expects. "Follow me (can anyone say more) and you shall have the light of life."

Breadth is a quality of God's mercy, not a hall-mark of man's iniquity; it is not the insignia of inefficiency, but the one essential quality of that wisdom which can lead to final achievement. It has always been to me one of the great claims of Christ Himself to be something more than an ordinary man, that in His tiny, circumscribed stage on earth, with His intense idealism, devoted purpose, and matchless courage, He could be the broadest in His judgments of any religious Leader the world has ever known.

A journey through the old civilisation of Egypt, up into the Sudan, impressed upon us how men exactly like ourselves, for thousands of years have been passing across the same stage as we, in endless, unceasing numbers, generation after generation, race after race, century after century. Everywhere one sees in the most indestructible materials they knew of the evidences that their greatest desire was to secure permanence for themselves at any cost, in every possible way of which they could conceive. Moreover, they have so far rendered permanent their bodies on earth that we looked into their very faces, six thousand years after they had passed on, and pictured as clearly what they did and said and thought as if we verily were mixing again among the living actors on their own stage of life. As we gazed into the face of the old King Amenhotep IV lying in his tomb just as he was put there thousands of years ago, and at the bodies of his servants killed at the same time that their souls might go with him for service in the next world, we realised how that desire is universal and natural and is our best hope that it will be satisfied.

It is the same all around the globe, wherever man crawls upon its surface. We passed through another great cradle of mankind, the valleys of the Tigris and Euphrates. Here again all around us were written the same lessons as on the Nile. At

Ur of the Chaldees, the home of Abraham, at Kish, oldest of known great cities, at Babylon, famous for the wonderful men who ruled the world of their day, at a hundred ancient haunts of mankind, is inscribed the same verdict. So strong was his desire for permanent life that man, coming into these then fertile plains from the high mountains, was not satisfied to express his devotion by mere temples rising from the ground, though these were buildings that took years to erect like our own great cathedrals. But God was so unattainable that He must obviously be worshipped from that which was really high, and not a Temple merely called so. So these started by first building a mountain on the plain. The ziggurats, or artificial hills, which they raised to place their temples upon, took so long to erect that the workers who commenced the task could seldom have expected to see its completion. Their zeal, their devotion, their sacrifices were boundless.

Yet all these greatest conceptions of man are alike brought to nought by that dimension of our universe which we are just beginning to recognise as an integral part of all our science — the fourth dimension of time. So we know it will be with all our "things," all our "permanent" buildings, all our provisions for getting, keeping, holding, all will be as futile as those of Seti or Rameses, or Urgengur, or Nebuchadnezzar; exactly as was the case of our infinitely more ancient fellow men, who left flint knives which we picked up after they had been buried deep beneath the very foundation of Kish itself, or of the other men who left their arrow heads in the sands on the top of the ancient Egyptian highlands probably before the Nile ever existed — to say nothing of their ancestors who crawled their earth in a yet earlier day, and of whom all traces are lost far back in the aeons of geologic time.

It is obvious that man is himself a traveller; that the purpose of this world is not "to have and to hold" but to "give and to serve." There can be no other meaning. The lesson of the time element of our cosmogony, of the temporary duration of things, far from discouraging us from effort should spur us to truer and nobler and more earnest work, because not in the thing but in our activity lies the road to our real completion and permanence. We are spiritual beings, not material ones, and the meaning of life is its spiritual value, and our unselfishness is the pledge of the better day that awaits us. Even the exact, emotionless sciences of mathematics, chemistry and physics are today suggesting that the atom itself has no material substance whatever. But there are two things that no true and wise man will deny: namely, that love is the greatest thing in the world, and that "he loveth best who serveth best." What greater thing can Christ mean to any generation of the world than these truths? Was not the whole lesson of His life that here not even He, as expressed through His physical body, had "any abiding city." Life is obviously a school, not a bargain counter. Yet so real a counter is it, that the pride and pleasure of winning out in the transaction is entrusted to us ourselves to win or lose. So great are the possibilities of it that so far it has been a sheer impossibility for it to have entered into the heart of man to conceive what awaits those who love God "in the spirit that Christ revealed to us" as possible. Doubt this of course we will, but it is scientifically true that it is as far beyond our brain conception as the thoughts suggested by the new knowledge of matter, each atom of which is now known to be a universe with planets called electrons flying in their orbits round a central proton. Thus hydrogen has one planet, but gold no less than seventy-nine in every atom, suggesting that our sun and all its planets including our earth may be but an atom of some infinitely great substance in a universe, the size of which no human mind could ever conceive.

Yet these things are not to discourage, but to reassure us; not to drive us to despair and make us content to hand over our divine spark of reason either to unthinking superstition or to shallow claimants to infallible intelligence; but to inspire our faith with that basis of reason which it has a right to demand and certainly longs for; namely, that there are bigger things than our little brain can even imagine, and that comprehension is no limit to legitimate acceptance of axioms. Prayer is not to inform God of what He does not know. It is an eye through which we see God. Faith is not a denial of reason, it is a corollary of finality in relation with the infinite.

Travelling in the Holy Land itself teaches, as perhaps nothing else on earth could teach, that fatal propensity of mankind to fix his heart and mind not on realities, but on the shadows called things; and so ever to meet disappointment in life, as he finds at the hands of the greatest of all teachers — experience — what phantoms are all that he has thought real. In the innumerable piles of tinsel heaped everywhere in profusion on what are called "sacred sites," it seems as though the enemy of mankind had determined by mere momentum of atomic weight to keep down the Spirit that once came to earth in the Master of men, and to hide for ever beneath "things" the real vision of men as spiritual beings and sons of God.

On Christmas Eve, at Bethlehem, somewhere in the neighbourhood of the Nativity of Christ, "under the wide and starry sky," we gathered a motley crowd, like that which assembles on Christmas Eve in England or Beacon Hill in Boston on the same occasion, to rejoice in the vision then given to man of his great destiny. It was rather cold, and the flickering candles made it difficult to read the words of the time-honored old carols. It was a real delight to have things put in their place for once; for somehow there was impressed on everyone's heart the inherent simplicity of the truth, and the real miracle of "the Way" in which that truth had been taught to men. Here we were standing on the spot which more than any other on all the round globe for twenty centuries has influenced the progress of the world towards what mankind at its best is striving for. Here the true nature of love was revealed through the physical life of a village Carpenter, a life that ended on a felon's Cross. Yet here, under such circumstances, had the world been taught that man's life on earth is not a hopeless tragedy, but that physical life here can be for us all just an abiding field of honour; that reality is not in the armour, the sword, or the plumes, but in the spirit; and that without the incoming and indwelling of that Spirit no intellectual infallibility, no meticulous ritual, no self-deprivation of talents which are given to man to spell for him capacity and responsibility, nothing mental, nothing physical, can proclaim what Christ means to any one life or to mankind.

As we there faced the question of what Christ intended He should mean to each of us, what in our heart of hearts could we be conscious of as the true answer, fear though we might to confess it, and dread though we might to face it? What does He mean? It can be no demand that we understand Him. Still less that we should consent to recognize Him. Can it be less than a challenge to follow Him?

Men of every age, of every clime, of every race, have longed for a solution of life's riddle. What is the meaning of life on earth? The answer that rings out to the ages from the life of Jesus Christ is not a dope or a maudlin soporific. It is a challenge as clear as the sun at midday: "Follow me."

No man has ever done despite to his reason or his faith by his willingness to take up that challenge. The school of experience is the one in which men themselves, especially men who accomplish things, place most confidence. In surgery and medicine we are obliged by our Colleges to stand by our "end results." That is what Christ asked. Have any who have ever answered that challenge "*sans peur et sans raproche*" ever been deceived? To whom today in the light of history would the increasing wisdom of the world award the mead of having chosen most wisely? This is part of what Christ has meant to me.

Chess is the king of games. Its great squares leading across the board to the spot where every pawn may win a crown, have always fascinated me. The sinister picture of God and the Devil moving the pawns about without their being consulted almost ruined it for me. But when Alice in her Wonderland wandered across my pathway, and I saw that the pieces moved themselves, the game became again to me a helpful parable. It enabled me to visualise somewhat the interest of Him, Whom I think of as watching its millions of pieces throughout the ages, as they work out their own destinies in the drama of life. When first I visited Labrador, there was no lighthouse on its rock-bound coast, so a friend offered both the money to build one, and the salary of a keeper. However, the Government warned us that no private person may own a lighthouse, for possibly the man might let its light go out. Every year, with a thousand other vessels, I cruise along our rugged coastline. Each vessel sets out full of high hopes of a successful voyage, a full fare, and afterward a hearty "well done" from the satisfied owner of the craft, when at the end of the venture she has once more reached home. Alas! Our coast is strewn with wrecks. How many times have I sorely needed a pilot and guide myself to advise me what to do! How often have I struck my beloved little ship, because the coast pilot that was all the guide we had, could not be depended upon.

We have been badly handicapped in our work for children, especially for the unfortunate tuberculous lying under the shadow of the Valley of Death, by the difficulty of letting the sunshine in, and at the same time keeping out the biting winds and raw cold from our Polar current. The ordinary glass we use for our windows oddly enough prevents the vital rays of the sun from passing through, though it is apparently clear and translucent. Our bodies, sorely in need, look out for these rays but are betrayed, for little of value to human life comes through the windows. Lying on my table is a substance called Vitaglass. It shields from danger and gives life-giving light at the same time.

Faith came to me with the vision of Christ still alive in this world today. I owe it to Him. He meant to me a determination, God helping me, to follow Him. Whither it led me I have tried to outline in this booklet. Certain it is that a life among fishermen was the last place I should have sought at twenty years of age with my background. Not one of my chums selected anything like it. I have tried to subordinate my will to

His, and to play across the board as if He were directing my share in the game. True, my five senses have never made me conscious of His physical presence in hours of temptation, fear, discouragement, and doubt; but there are other senses to be relied upon, whether physical or spiritual I cannot say, because as a matter of fact neither I nor any man knows the difference. Thus I can account for but cannot see, touch, hear, smell, or taste the force which makes my compass needle point towards the North except when deflected by some local mundane stronger line; nor can I account for or my senses perceive why baby seals always beat North in the dark frigid waters beneath the Arctic ice fields, nor how polar bears and migrating birds follow tracks which no mortal man can follow without outside help. All I know is that they get there.

The process of knowing one's self is a painful one. I remember undertaking to paint the ceiling in our new hospital sitting room because I thought I could do it without staining the floor or the walls. I did my very best, but alas! not only my friends but I myself were conscious of many stains made through my own fault. Moreover, glue had dropped into my own hair, and certainly I did not wish that. We all need a pilot stronger and better and braver and truer than ourselves and experience teaches us of none who can compare with the Christ.

In this respect, what has Christ meant to me? Christ who was the Man of all others who did things. Stanley Jones, in his *Christ of the Indian Road*, exactly depicts my own conception of Him. Our Lord, he says, did not spend much time speculating or talking or writing books. He worked at the carpenter's bench. He fought temptation in the wilderness and put prayer into action. He healed the sick. He cast out devils. He wept with His friends. He treated women on an equality. Girt with a towel, He washed the feet of fishermen. He personally went and mixed and ate with outcasts. He began His preaching at home. He transformed weak, ignorant, selfish and cowardly men into heroes. He Himself brought heaven to earth wherever He was. His answer to John's disciples was "Go and tell what you see done." He fed the hungry, visited the sick. Even His personal clothing He let go; when men smote Him, He turned the other cheek. He willingly walked all the way to Jerusalem, conscious that He was going to His Cross, so that on it He might bear the burdens of all other men. He was acquainted with sorrows. That made Him capable of being always the man who could smile; and He would weep also, and knew well how to laugh. He must have loved the repartee so wonderfully characteristic of His wisdom that he has stood the test of ages. What a twinkle there must have been in His eyes!

If I don't understand how He walked on the water or how He raised the dead, I am perfectly content to pass on and wait to comprehend those things when I shall have acquired more wisdom than now. God forbid that I should try to circumscribe the genius of greater men than I by the limits of my imperfect cerebral cells. I do not wish to be numbered with the mob who persecuted Galileo, fought Pasteur, tried to kill Lord Lister, drove Morton into his grave, pooh-poohed heavier-than-air aviation, ridiculed automobiles and even steam railways, sneered at Dr. Bell and his telephone dream as a lunatic, and refused to help the discoveries of radium and X-rays until those efforts took the form of dividend-paying shares on the stock market. "The mark of greatness," said Gladstone, "is not how little, but how much, a man believes in."

How does such a Christ help to reconsecration? He helps by setting the highest possible standards in Himself, by actually challenging us to look at Him and daring us to follow Him. That is the way to inspire mankind. That is what Christ has done for me, a thousand times. Were I to hear Him say once to the fallen women or to the traitor Judas, "Go to hell with your sins," or threaten punishment to His weakest follower, then it would all be different. I can understand His saying to the man who definitely refused to do anything with his talent, putting it away from beyond his reach by burying it till his death, "Take it away from him." I understand a

173

righteous judge summing up a closed life judicially by saying, "You did nothing to help anyone; neither the naked, the hungry, the sick, the down-and-outs, not even the children. Go to the place prepared for the Devil." Such living is a negation of life. That is why also I can understand a plan of redemption which calls for any sacrifice for love, especially the divine love of which there is no fathoming the depth. Yes, it makes intelligible that which, for want of any better way of expressing it in human language, we call "the sacrifice of God's only Son." That too, Christ means to me. I am conscious that for me my only hope of salvation in this world lies in Christ.

The faith in Christ upon which I have based my life has given me a light on life's meaning which has satisfied my mind, body, and soul. The hope that through that faith, He would reveal a way of life here which justifies it, has been more than answered; and it seems to me ever more reasonable to hold that it will "carry on," just as gloriously when we have passed beyond the limits of what material machines can reveal to us. That the love which has made itself conscious to me though forty-odd years and has not failed even when I failed, should desert me when in the presence of God I shall need it most is to me unthinkable. No. I don't know what redemption means, but knowing myelf, I cannot avoid realising the necessity for it, nor can I see any reason why my glad acceptance of faith in the only way I ever heard of should offend my intellect because I do not fully understand it.

Humility is an essential of all true science. Why not in this, the greatest of all? Pharpar and Abana are denied me. Am I foolish because I accept the Waters of Jordan?

"He who would valiant be
    'Gainst all disaster,
Let him in constancy
    Follow the Master.
There's no discouragement
    Shall make him once relent;

His firm avowed intent
To be a Christian."

BUNYAN

Books by Wilfred Grenfell

Vikings of Today (Marshall, London, 1895, 1986 and Revell, N.Y., 1896).

The Harvest of the Sea (Revell, London, Toronto, 1905).

Newfoundland Guidebook (Bradbury Agnew, London, 1905).

Off the Rocks: Stories of the Deep Sea Fishermen of Labrador (Sunday School Times, Philadelphia, 1906 and Books For Libraries, Freeport, N.Y., 1970).

A Bit of Autobiography (Grenfell Association of America, N.Y., 1907).

A Man's Faith (Pilgrim, Boston, 1908, 1926 and Marshall, London, 1909).

A Voyage on an Ice Pan (Pilgrim, Boston, 1908 and Ellis, Boston, 1908).

Adrift on an Ice Pan (Copp Clark, Toronto, 1909; Melrose, London, 1909; Houghton Mifflin, N.Y., Boston, 1909, 1911, 1914, 1923, 1925, 1926, 1929, 1937; and Constable, London, 1910).

Down to the Sea: Yarns from the Labrador (Revell, N.Y., London, Toronto, 1910 and Melrose, London, 1910).

177

A Man's Helper (Pilgrim, Boston, 1910).

Labrador, The Country and the People (Macmillan, N.Y., 1910).

What Life Means to Me (Pilgrim, Boston, N.Y., 1910 and Nisbett, London, 1918).

What Will You Do With Jesus Christ? (Pilgrim, Boston, N.Y., 1910, 1911).

Down North on the Labrador (Revell, N.Y., 1911 and Nisbett, Toronto, 1912).

The Adventure of Life (Nisbett, London, 1912 and Pilgrim, Boston, N.Y., 1913).

On Immortality (Pilgrim, Boston, 1912 and Nisbett, London, 1913).

Shall A Man Live Again? (Pilgrim, N.Y., Boston, 1912).

What Can Jesus Christ Do For Me? (Pilgrim, Boston, N.Y., 1912).

The Attractive Way (McClelland and Goodchild, Toronto, 1913 and Pilgrim, Boston, 1913).

The Prize of Life (Pilgrim, Boston, 1914).

Tales of the Labrador (Houghton Mifflin, Boston, N.Y., 1916 and Nisbett, London, 1917).

Labrador Days (Houghton Mifflin, Boston, 1919; Hodder and Stoughton, London, 1921; and Books For Libraries, Freeport, N.Y., 1971).

A Labrador Doctor (Houghton Mifflin, Boston, 1919, 1925, 1929 and Hodder and Stoughton, London, 1920, 1921). Republished with new material as *Forty Years for Labrador*.

Northern Neighbors (Houghton Mifflin, Boston, 1923, 1924 and Hodder and Stoughton, London, 1923).

That Christmas in Peace Harbour (Houghton Mifflin, Boston, 1923).

Labrador and Newfoundland: an Outline History of the Work of the International Grenfell Association (s.n., Boston, 1924 and A.G. Co., Boston, 1926).

Yourself and Your Body (Copp Clark, Toronto, 1924; Charles Scribner's Sons, N.Y., 1924; and Hodder and Stoughton, London, 1924, 1925).

Religion in Everyday Life (American Library Association, Chicago, 1926).

What Christ Means to Me (Houghton Mifflin, N.Y., 1927 and Hodder and Stoughton, London, 1926, 1928, 1932, 1956).

Labrador Looks At the Orient (Jarrolds, London, 1928 and Houghton Mifflin, Boston, 1928).

Labrador's Fight for Economic Freedom (Benn, London, 1929).

The Fisherman's Saint (Hodder and Stoughton, London, 1930).

The Story of a Labrador Doctor (Hodder and Stoughton, London, 1931).

Forty Years for Labrador (Houghton Mifflin, Boston, 1932 and Hodder and Stoughton, London, 1932, 1933, 1934).

The Romance of Labrador (Macmillan, N.Y., 1934 and Hodder and Stoughton, London, 1934).

Deeds of Daring (Hodder and Stoughton, London, 1934).

Labrador Log Book (Houghton Mifflin, Boston, 1938; Little Brown, Boston, 1938, 1940; McClelland and Stewart, Toronto, 1938; and Hodder and Stoughton, London, 1939).

Books Edited by Wilfred Grenfell
Book of Newfoundland, By Great Waters, Great Canadian Adventure Stories, Harbor Tales Down North, Openings, Passages.

Magazines That Published Articles by Wilfred Grenfell
Boston Transcript, Canadian Magazine, Journal of National Institute of Social Science, National Geographic.